HOW TO
RUN
A QUIZ

Also available from *Elliot Right Way Books*

Ready-Made Quizzes
The Quiz-Setter's Quiz Book
Quirky Quiz Questions

All uniform with this book

HOW TO RUN A QUIZ

COMPILED BY
DAVE CORNISH

RIGHT WAY

Typeset in 10/12pt Times by County Typesetters, Margate, Kent.

Printed and bound in Great Britain by Cox & Wyman Ltd., Reading, Berkshire.

The *Right Way series* is published by Elliot Right Way Books, Brighton Road, Lower Kingswood, Tadworth, Surrey, KT20 6TD, U.K. For information about our company and the other books we publish, visit our web site at www.right-way.co.uk

CONTENTS

With thanks to Marcia Rapacioli, Tim Fitt, Steve Ling
and all my friends in the Enfield Library Service for their
help and assistance, and especially to Anne, my wife,
without whom I would never have got round to it at all.

1

INTRODUCTION

The Popularity of Quizzes
Radio and television are continually spawning new quiz games as well as persevering with old favourites. Organisations as diverse as the Women's Institute and the local rugby club organise quizzes for social and/or fund-raising purposes. Most households now seem to possess quiz-related games along the lines of 'Trivial Pursuit'. Quiz leagues are operating all over the country, and even the pubs have latched on to their commercial possibilities by installing cash-paying quiz machines to stand alongside their more traditional fruit machines.

Why are quizzes so popular? It cannot be the thrill of winning, for inevitably most participants end up as also-rans. To my mind, taking part in a quiz is not merely entertaining in itself but, win or lose, many people appear to derive an intense satisfaction from knowing the answer to a tricky question and get a feeling of smugness by knowing at least one answer which somebody else did not!

An example to illustrate this point. The popularity of television's 'Mastermind' format with contestants being given two minutes to answer questions on a specialist topic of their own choosing and two minutes of general knowledge questions. Whilst it is certainly true that its popularity might in part be ascribed to 'hype' (from the foreboding music accompanying the opening credits to the idea of an isolated 'interrogation chair' in the spotlight) one would have thought that other parts of its format would have detracted from its popularity. After all, the specialist subjects chosen have often been obscure, and the standard of general knowledge questions significantly more difficult than in most other quiz programmes. Indeed, I suspect that the average viewer could answer relatively few.

Yet it has worked. The series first started as long ago as 1972, with viewing figures consistently rivalling those of what is normally considered popular (and thus accessible) entertainment. Personally, I put much of its success down to the one-upmanship displayed by the armchair viewer who knew an answer that the poor person in the spotlight did not.

Taking part in a quiz should be fun. However, you cannot *force* people to have fun. Whether or not they enjoy the quiz is up to them, but a well-arranged quiz with fair and interesting questions should reduce the chances of complaint and enhance the likelihood that they will enjoy themselves.

What makes a *good* quiz? From one point of view a quiz is good when all the participants leave knowing that – win or lose – they have enjoyed themselves. If they felt that it was in any way 'unfair' – and that could mean that the questions were badly phrased, that one team were asked an easier set of questions than they were, or (unforgiveable!) that the answers you gave were dubious – then this would detract from their enjoyment. As far as you are concerned, a good quiz is one where not only have the participants had a good time, but where the total organisation was such that there were no hitches and, hopefully, you had a good time too.

Arranging a good quiz does need careful planning. It is essential to decide well in advance the format of the quiz (is it to be a knockout competition? will individuals be expected to answer questions individually or by conferring? how much time should be allowed to answer each question? etc.) as well as compiling a set of questions which are appropriate both to the format of the quiz and to those taking part. All of this demands planning and considerable work in advance but it should be fun. If the intention is for the participants to have fun there is no reason why the person arranging the quiz should not have fun too!

The Layout of this Book

The purpose of this book is to offer you guidance in running a quiz and, hopefully, to help you avoid some of the pitfalls that could otherwise mar your efforts. No advice is offered on the domestic arrangements concerned e.g. the hire of suitable premises, the pricing and selling of tickets, the provision of refreshments etc. However, do not leave anything to chance. These decisions and arrangements are just as important in your planning; for example an error in hiring a small room and then selling tickets to over 100 contestants would reduce the quiz to a débacle before you had even started. Make sure that you have everything under control at all times.

Running a quiz is more than just thinking up a certain number of questions – that is the final stage. Until you have determined how the quiz is to be operated, do not start compiling a set of questions, as these may not be appropriate.

Chapter Two covers the format of the quiz and ends with detailed explanations of some of the more common formats used. It is of course entirely up to you whether you wish to adopt or adapt one of these, or whether you wish to apply the more general points made and to devise your own format.

Chapter Four offers guidance in compiling a set of questions appropriate to the format chosen and directs you towards sources of inspiration. It also offers advice on phrasing questions for maximum impact and indicates some of the unexpected problems that may otherwise arise.

Chapters Five (and Six) contain sample questions (and answers) on different subjects which I have used at various quizzes of differing standards. They are included not necessarily because I would advise you to use them but because they offer examples of the *types* of question which could be asked and may therefore offer you some ideas.

One final point I should make is that there is no reason why the quizmaster – who I refer to throughout as the 'QM' – must be male. My dictionary defines the term as 'a *person* who puts questions to contestants . . .'. This task can be accomplished as well (or as badly!) by anyone, regardless of sex.

2
QUIZ FORMATS

It is obviously not a good idea to arrange a quiz evening and to go along armed with hundreds of questions if you have no idea who is going to be asked what, when, how etc. Organising a quiz involves far more than just setting the questions. It also involves determining the format of the quiz – the rules and procedure necessary for its efficient conduct – so that ultimately a winner (or winners) can be declared.

Ideally the format of the quiz should be such that all contestants feel that it is 'fair', that they enjoy taking part, and, hopefully, that you are able to enjoy it as well. Different people have different concepts of fairness (I have met many who genuinely felt that it was unfair that they were asked questions they did not know the answers to!) but realistically a 'fair' quiz is one in which, at least at the outset, all contestants have an equal chance of winning and will only be prevented from doing so by their inability to answer as many questions correctly as other contestants (or by their inability to answer them as quickly).

It is also important that you arrange the quiz in such a manner that you are not beset by too many problems during the course of it. Such precautions as ensuring that there is adequate seating or remembering to bring all the essential parts of your equipment really lie outside the scope of this book, although they are vital nonetheless. Sit down well in advance of the occasion and visualise what is needed. It may seem a waste of time but could save trials and tribulations later!

Whichever format you decide upon, always ensure that all

contestants understand the rules *before* you start asking any questions. It can be very disruptive if there are any arguments or queries over the rules during the course of the quiz itself.

It is well worthwhile to try out a new format on some friends beforehand – it may well throw up some problems you had overlooked and these can then be sorted out before the event.

Whilst I have concluded this chapter with examples of some of the more common formats used for quizzes, you can adapt parts of them or even invent your own. The points made below are merely for guidance; I would suggest you consider them whilst determining the precise format your quiz will take.

A contest between individuals or between teams?
The first thing to decide is whether the quiz should involve individuals competing against other individuals or whether it should be a team contest. Already we have a problem: if it is to be a team contest, should there be any part of it when an individual team member is 'put in the spotlight' and expected to answer a question without the assistance of other team members?

Always bear in mind the purpose of the quiz. If the contest is, for example, intended to produce a champion individual – 'Mastermind of the Crown and Horseshoes' or 'Brain of the Davies Family' – then obviously you have already decided on an individual contest. However, this type of contest may prove to be less popular as many people are reluctant to take part for fear of embarrassing themselves should they not be able to answer many questions.

Contests between individuals usually demand slightly 'easier' questions (whatever that might mean!) as a team conferring over an answer are likely to be able to supplement the knowledge of one individual. In my experience I have found that the spread of marks (from the top to the bottom contestant) is larger with a contest between individuals than it is between teams. This may reflect the fact that some individuals naturally retain the sort of information necessary to perform well at quizzes, and/or the fact that a team acting together to produce an answer can iron out an individual's deficiency of knowledge in some areas.

If the quiz is intended as a social occasion (which I suspect most are), then you should endeavour to involve all participants throughout the quiz. The elimination of people at an early stage will obviously detract from their enjoyment and tend to make the session less of a success socially, so do ask yourself whether a knock-out format really is the most suitable.

Wherever possible, my preference is for team events as they tend to attract a larger number of participants. Many people seem to feel some sense of identity with the rest of their team – whether it be a pub, an office, or just a group of friends – and they are often able to persuade people to join their team who would not have chosen to participate had it been a contest for individuals.

Written or oral?
If your quiz is participatory (not intended for spectators) then there is no reason why answers cannot be written rather than spoken; however, this is somewhat boring for spectators who want to know what is going on throughout and need to be kept entertained. If the quiz is being operated as a spectator event, then the whole quiz must be operated on a verbal basis.

Speed v Knowledge
For those quizzes which seek to determine the breadth of an individual's or team's knowledge, sufficient time should be allowed for consideration or conferring. In this type of quiz contestants are not put under severe time pressure and are allowed a reasonable time (at least 20 seconds) to come up with an answer.

More exciting for spectators, though, is where *speed* is at least as important as knowledge: contestants are put under extreme time pressure, usually by beating other contestants to a buzzer. This type of quiz may well penalize the more ponderous types but can offer great fun for contestants and spectators alike.

Remember that you should not continue asking a question once a contestant has pressed their buzzer but invite an immediate answer, penalizing undue hesitation as if it were an incorrect answer by deducting points. If you were to continue asking a question once a buzzer had been pressed you would be encouraging contestants to press before they knew the answer in the knowledge that they would have time to consider their answer whilst the remainder of the question was being read out and that they had, in effect, 'frozen out' their opponents by depriving them of the opportunity of answering.

Should questions answered incorrectly be offered to the other contestant(s) to answer for a bonus point? Bear in mind that if you have deducted points for an incorrect answer, then the other contestant has already benefited. On the other hand, if you decide that the question should be offered for a bonus it is only fair to repeat the question *in full*, but not to allow too much time for an answer to be forthcoming as this could destroy the fast tempo of the quiz.

If you are running a quiz which uses buzzers, allow contestants to interrupt. In some quizzes (including some on television) contestants must wait for the question to be completed before buzzing. This often leads to a race to press the buzzer first, and it may well be that the contestant who thought of the answer first is beaten to the buzzer by another contestant who only came upon the answer right at the end of the question.

Who gets asked which question?
All contestants like to know that the quiz is 'fair'. If everyone is asked the same set of questions then you have gone a long way to achieving this, but this is not always possible.

Suggestions:
— If you ask everyone the same question *either* they write their answers down on paper *or* it becomes a race against time to see who presses a buzzer first (or whatever other form of indication is used).
— Invariably, if contestants are asked different questions (e.g. one person/team is asked question A and a second person/team is asked question B) everyone believes they

have been asked a 'harder' set of questions. This is something that cannot be avoided. Try to alleviate the problem and to demonstrate that any bias that they have discerned was unintentional. It is often wise to make a play of shuffling the set of questions in plain view of everyone (if you have them written on individual cards) or by tossing a coin to decide who gets the first question. Or use any method which proves that it is not pre-ordained which person/team gets asked which set of questions.

— In any type of quiz where questions are addressed to a particular team (or individual) be careful about allowing that question to 'go on offer' should it not be answered correctly. If there are more than two teams participating, how do you decide *who* should get that opportunity? After all, it would hardly be fair automatically to offer it to the team on their left, say, as there would be a marked advantage in sitting to the left of the weakest team.

Using a PA system

However loud and clear you may think your voice is, it is surprising how much it will suffer from background chatter amongst spectators and/or contestants. For all but the very intimate, homely, type of quiz, you would be well advised to consider using a PA system both to project your voice and to gain attention. Talking through a PA system seems to command a degree of respect and authority and may well quieten people down prior to the asking of questions.

Some premises have their own PA systems; if not, they can be hired fairly cheaply from a range of companies listed in the local Yellow Pages. The cost of hire should be weighed up against the problems which might otherwise be encountered such as having virtually to shout each question on the more boisterous occasions.

Using a microphone appears to frighten some people but if used properly it is simplicity itself. The knack is to speak slowly and clearly (good advice for a QM with or without a microphone) and to imagine that you are explaining something to a single stranger. Do not be taken in by singers on TV who appear to hold their microphones at arm's length. Most PA systems use a different type of microphone, and it is often necessary to hold it quite close to your mouth (though take care *not* to let it actually touch your lips: it could prove very dangerous if it was not properly earthed!). Practising your microphone technique is useful but remember that as the room fills up it may be necessary to increase the volume.

More sophisticated PA systems may include tape-deck facilities, which may spur you into considering asking questions about pieces of music played (I have heard this expanded to include rounds involving identifying sounds, guessing the name of the celebrity talking and, on one occasion, naming the ten languages that a passage was read in!).

Use of the tape-deck in this way certainly adds a new dimension to any quiz and is a break from the monotony of asking and answering purely verbal questions but you should be aware of some of the drawbacks:

— If anything should go wrong and the tape fails to work you *must* have an emergency verbal round to ask. After all, if the PA system breaks down you could always (at a pinch) shout, but if the expected music fails to work you are hardly going to sing!

— Most tapes can be prepared fairly easily on a domestic sound system but when played at a greater volume than was intended and through an amplifier and speakers that were primarily designed purely for speech, the results can be awfully distorted.

— When recording, decide how long each piece of music is to last and how much gap you should leave between one track and the next. If, for example, each track lasts 25 seconds, then you may care to take a 5 second gap between tracks and switch the tape deck off at the end of each track to ask the next question before re-starting the tape-deck. Avoid recording the question itself (because of the possibility of distortion) and of leaving a longer (say 20 second) gap between tracks in which to ask the next question whilst the tape is still running (lest the end of the question asked is

drowned by the next track starting).
— Beware of the difficulties inherent in repeating tracks. This
would involve rewinding the tape, and it may be difficult to
stop rewinding at the appropriate point.

Displaying the scores

Spectators and contestants alike will need to be reminded of the
latest scores on a regular basis. This can be done verbally at
regular intervals for small-scale quizzes with very few participants but this is blatantly not feasible if this were to amount to
two or three dozen. It would probably take as long to read out
the scores after a round of questions as to read out the questions
themselves!

Plan in advance how you propose to display the scores. Some
premises may have suitable equipment which you could use, for
example if the quiz was being held at a school you may have
access to a blackboard. If possible, check the facilities in
advance and take with you whatever you may need.

Scores need to be displayed in a position where they can be
seen by all concerned, should be updated as quickly as possible,
and constructed in such a way that this updating is neither too
difficult nor disruptive. Displaying scores is not always such an
easy job as it might appear. If there are many individuals/teams
participating then it is unrealistic to expect the QM to do it as
well. If you have sufficient assistance you ought to consider
persuading someone to take charge of the scoring, or ask
someone who is marking written questions to double up.

For quizzes contested by two individuals or teams it may be
possible to use a ring binder approach whereby, for example,
the numbers 1 to 50 are written large on separate sheets of card,
then punched and bound. These are fastened securely to the
edge of a table, and as each question is answered correctly a
card is flipped over the edge of the table revealing the latest
score for that person or team.

The more technically-minded may consider using items such
as overhead projectors, if they are available. These work by
writing the scores on an acetate which are magnified and
projected on a screen. Beware though, for not only are they

ineffective in bright conditions (your holiday slides are not easy to view in daylight) but you may also find that the premises which you are using has no suitable surface on which to project.

An alternative to using a blackboard is to come along armed with a large sheet of white card (at least A1 size) already ruled up to display the marks as they become available, and a thick black marker pen. Again, this is not without its dangers as you always have to find a reasonably accessible flat area on which to fit it. If you are unable to find out in advance anything about the premises, then at the very least go along with sellotape, drawing pins and blu-tack, and preferably a board and easel as well!

One of the more exotic (but no less effective) methods of displaying the scores I have come across was an occasion when the organiser had draped a washing line round the walls and the scores were displayed on sheets of paper attached by pegs! It turned out to be a somewhat labour intensive affair, but it did serve a useful function in keeping three youngsters occupied.

Whichever method you decide upon, make sure that you have the necessary equipment with you, that people detailed to assist know what they have to do and that it is accomplished as quickly and efficiently as possible. Do keep a handwritten master score sheet as it may be difficult to correct any errors if you do not have ready access to the scoresheet.

Marking answers

Deciding whether answers are correct or not should, wherever possible, be the responsibility of just one person in order to establish consistency. In the case of quizzes where answers are given verbally this needs to be the QM as a quick decision is needed but if answers are written, a different set of circumstances applies.

However attractive it may appear, *never* allow one team/ person to mark the answers of another. It is often tempting as you have a ready supply of labour to do a necessary job and non-participating volunteers may be difficult to find, but the problems it creates can be overwhelming. Imagine a quiz with 30 teams each submitting 10 written answers to a round of questions. If these were to be redistributed to other teams to

mark you may well suffer some or all of the following
difficulties:

— There is loss of tempo. It takes time to go through this
   stage, and participants may well complain that they came
   for a quiz, not to do the marking.
— It tends to be disruptive, with teams trying to find out from
   other teams whether they have accepted certain answers as
   correct.
— There is less likely to be consistency. One team may accept
   an answer as correct, whilst another adjudges it incorrect.
— Written answers are often not as you expect. You are likely
   to be asked for individual advice on some answers, for
   example 'which horse, trained by Jimmy Frost, won the
   1989 Grand National?' [A – 'Little Polveir'] may well invite
   queries from teams who have to decide whether 'Big
   Polveir' is acceptable.

To gain consistency in marking written answers it is best to
have one person alone detailed to perform this function,
supplied with a list of answers with any key words that must
appear in the answer underlined. For most questions which
involve naming an individual, it is the surname which is
important, and thus it is the surname which is underlined. If a
team selects the wrong Christian names I would not usually
penalize them – particularly as other teams may well only
answer with a surname.

As marking written answers can be time-consuming, it is
often advisable for the QM not to be involved directly, possibly
doing no more than making a decision on any borderline
answers turned up by the marker(s).

SOME TRIED AND TESTED QUIZ FORMATS

1. The 'Social Quiz'
This is a popular form of team quiz and is particularly widely
used for fund-raising purposes. It is called a social quiz as
everyone is involved throughout (no-one is eliminated) and in

many ways the quiz is merely a catalyst for a social occasion as each team confers over all of their answers.

Each team consists of an equal number of people, usually between 4 and 10 depending on the size of the tables and the premises available. At the outset, each team is given a team name (or number), a written team question (see below) and a sufficient supply of blank answer sheets. The QM commences by briefly explaining the procedure and in particular stressing that only one answer per team is required but that they may well need to confer (argue?) in order to decide their answer.

Other than the written team question all questions are asked orally by the QM and the answers are written down on the answer sheets supplied. Each team must endeavour to answer every question and all teams are asked the same set of questions.

After performing the introductions, the QM asks a round of questions on a particular subject ('general knowledge', 'travel', 'natural history', or whatever) allowing each team sufficient time to confer before writing down their answer. This process is continued until the end of the round, when a little extra time is allowed for second thoughts, last-minute inspiration or fine-tuning before all the answer sheets are collected.

Once all the answer sheets have been collected, the QM reads out the answers to that round and then continues by asking the questions from the second round. This procedure is continued until after the final round, when the results are announced and prizes awarded.

Delegate the task of marking to one or more people and supply them with a model answer sheet for each round and clear instructions, particularly as to what qualifies as a correct answer. The markers should write clearly on each answer sheet the total score obtained for that round and record these scores on a master scoresheet. This becomes important in case of complaint; it is amazing how often teams query their scores when in fact the fault lies with their own arithmetic.

The master scoresheet can then be used to transcribe the information on to the display scoreboard after reach round. If possible, delegate a separate person to be the scorer. As many participants seem to like consulting the scoreboard at the end of the quiz, ensure that the final scores are displayed.

The major variation from the above is the use of the written team question. This is handed out to each team at the start and contains one or more written questions which each team attempts to answer whilst simultaneously answering the various rounds of questions being asked orally. No time is allocated for this (the general idea is that they find time whilst deciding their answers to the other questions) but I would advise that they are handed in a few rounds before the end of the quiz as they can prove very time-consuming to mark.

As the team question tends to carry a reasonable proportion of the total number of marks available, it is best not to display these scores until the end of the contest in order to keep up an element of suspense. It is also advisable not to allocate too great a proportion of the total marks available to the team question as it may have the effect of negating the rest of the quiz. I have been to a quiz where the table question was worth the same number of points as all the oral questions combined. A team lying 20 points behind the leaders after the final oral round went on to win the quiz having scored 25 points more than any other merely by virtue of having an expert on that particular subject in their team. This made a mockery of the quiz and broke two of my rules for a good quiz – people enjoyed it less than they should have (it caused quite an uproar) and the majority did not regard it as 'fair'.

Another common variation to the social quiz is the inclusion of 'jokers'. At the outset each team is supplied with a 'joker' (usually a photocopied playing card joker with the name/ number of the team written on it) and a list of the titles of each round that are to be asked. Prior to asking the questions to each round the QM reminds each team of the title of the forthcoming round and asks whether any wish to 'play their joker'. Each team can play their joker once (and not for the written team question) with the result that their score for that round is doubled. It is therefore important that each round consists of the same number of questions.

Whilst admittedly more difficult to administer, it does have the advantage of continuing the uncertainty as to who is going to win and thus teams are more likely to continue their interest throughout.

One further 'optional extra' that you may consider including is a 'gamble question'. Teams are given five clues (usually one at the end of each of the first five rounds) and it becomes progressively easier to answer correctly as more clues are given.

Ten points are awarded to a team handing in a correct answer after hearing only one clue, eight points after hearing two clues and so on until only two points are awarded after all five clues have been read out.

An element of gambling is involved as teams have to weigh up whether it is worth risking their answer after very few clues in order to score more marks. Teams who answer correctly after hearing the fewest clues are rewarded by being credited with the most marks.

If you decide to include a 'gamble question', remember to issue each team with an extra – preferably coloured – answer paper, and encourage them to fold it before handing it in (to prevent other teams from seeing it). Mark it immediately so that you know just how many marks can be awarded but do not include those scores on the display scoreboard until all teams' answers have been marked.

Some words of advice:

— The number of rounds (and the number of questions in each of those rounds) depends on the amount of time available and how much time you allow for each question. As a rule of thumb, I find that ten rounds of ten questions each (even with a break for refreshments in the middle of the session) will take less than three hours.

— Try to set the rounds with a view to testing as wide a range of knowledge as possible. Ideally, each participant will be interested in at least some of the questions and ultimately the winning team will be the one that displays the best all-round knowledge. For example, there is no harm in asking a round of questions on Shakespeare, but why not then ask a round of questions on television? Equally, in a round of questions entitled 'music', why not include questions that may appeal to different people (and possibly people of different ages and interests) within the teams? For example, questions on Beethoven, Beiderbecke and the Beatles may well be answered by different members within each team.

— Announce in advance what procedure is to be adopted in the event of a tie as it is not unlikely that two or more teams will tie for the lead at the end of the evening and there is only one prize to be awarded. If there is likely to be sufficient time available, then an extra round of questions could be asked solely to those teams or an open ended question with each team invited to write down as many answers to a particular question as possible in 60 seconds. Giving teams 60 seconds to write down, say, as many US states beginning with the letter 'M' or as many of the actors who were part of the Magnificent Seven in the 1960 film of the same name, can often produce hectic activity – and fun – for teams participating in the tie break.

If time is likely to be short, then the only method is to recalculate the scores; firstly by discounting the joker round and if this fails to produce a winner, then discount the written round.

2.   The 'Pub Quiz'

This is a verbal contest between two teams of equal numbers, usually 3, 4 or 5 per team. The reason why I call it the 'pub quiz' is that this format (or something similar) is commonly used in pub quiz leagues across the country. It is relatively simple to administer and does not preclude an audience. However, as teams are asked different sets of questions this can lead to the complaint that one team was asked a 'harder' set of questions than the other team. This format also suffers from only being suitable for a contest between two teams, there being no adequate way of deciding which team should have the opportunity of answering an incorrectly answered question.

The QM sits at the front of the audience facing both teams, with one team on the left and the other on the right. Team members are seated together, usually behind tables and facing the audience.

The QM should sit alongside the scorer whose task it is to keep the score and read it out at the end of each round. This person usually doubles up as timer giving periodic warnings to each team of the elapsed time. For example, if it was decided to allow each team, say, thirty seconds to answer each question, the timer would start the stopwatch as soon as the QM has finished asking the question. After ten seconds had elapsed he would say 'ten', after twenty seconds he would say 'twenty'; and finally, if no answer was forthcoming he would say 'time up' or indicate this by banging a gavel or something to inform a team that they were timed out.

Some rounds are individual rounds in which a different question is posed to each team member in turn. A correct answer within the time limit scores that team two points, although if it is not answered correctly it is 'passed over' to the corresponding individual on the opposing team who earns a bonus point for their team by answering correctly.

The other rounds are team rounds in which both teams are asked questions. They may confer, and if the team captain gives the correct answer within the time limit, three points are awarded. If it is passed over to the other team they too may confer and two points are awarded provided the correct answer is given within the time limit.

Whilst it is not uncommon to allow both individuals and teams thirty seconds to provide an answer, this is usually reduced to, say, a further fifteen seconds if it is passed over. (An individual would already have had some time to consider the answer and a team should have conferred whilst awaiting for their opponents to answer). If an incorrect answer is given or 'time up' is signalled, the QM should invite the opposing team (or individual) to answer by naming them. This acts as a cue for the timer who then restarts the stopwatch.

It is a good idea to display the names of team members in front of them so that they can be seen by the audience and the QM. This makes it easier for the QM to address questions to a named individual ('Bill, what is the capital of . . .') which avoids any confusion as to who should be answering. Also, as each team member is 'paired' with someone from the opposing team, the other half of the 'pair' can be addressed by name should the question be passed over. Remember that this pairing system lasts throughout the quiz – e.g. if the second member of a team is unable to answer the question addressed to him, it is passed over to his 'pair' to answer (the second member of the opposing team).

As always, the total number of rounds will depend on the time available, but as a general rule a team round is usually used after two or three individual rounds and the final round is usually a team round.

The number of questions asked in a team round usually equals the number of members in each team, but there is no reason why this should not be extended such that, say, the final team round consists of ten or more questions.

3.   The 'Team' Quiz

This is best used for up to five teams, each team consisting of the same number of members (usually 3, 4 or 5) and as all questions and answers are oral spectators can attend.

Each team is seated in a row behind a table facing the QM (and the audience if there is one) with each member of each team numbered one, two, three, etc., (depending on the numbers in each team).

Other than the final round, each round is an 'individual round'. The quiz begins (after the QM has explained the rules to the participants) by the QM posing the first question to member number one of the first team. That person has the option of either attempting to answer it or of nominating another member of his own team to answer it by naming him (e.g. 'Bill Smith'). This individual may then either attempt to answer it or can nominate the team to answer it, by saying 'team'. No conferring is allowed unless the team are nominated to answer it.

If it is answered correctly by the individual to whom the question was addressed, the team scores three points. If it is answered correctly by another team member who was nominated, two points are awarded. One point is awarded to teams who have conferred before giving the correct answer.

If at any stage an incorrect answer is given, no points are awarded and no further attempts are allowed: the QM reads out the correct answer and moves on to asking the corresponding player of the next team a different question. Questions always remain within a team, and are never offered to other teams to answer. The round is concluded when each member of each team has had a question.

Whilst conferring is only allowed if a player has nominated the team to answer, this does not prevent other members of that team from indicating that they believe they know the answer by winking, smiling or in any way that could not lead to the impression that *answers* were being communicated. Of course there is no guarantee that a person indicating that he knows the answer really does!

To maintain the tempo of the quiz (and to put each team under a little pressure) the same length of time is allowed for each question to be answered – usually 30 seconds. An answer must be forthcoming within this time if it is to be valid, irrespective of whether it is answered for one, two or three points. If no answer is forthcoming within the allotted time limit, the QM announces the correct answer and moves on to ask the next question to the appropriate person (probably the corresponding member of the next team).

The number of individual rounds used will vary according to the envisaged length of the session, the number and size of teams and the amount of time allowed for each question to be answered. It is important, however, that each individual round is complete, in order that all members of each team have the same number of questions addressed to them.

The final round is a team round and during this round teams may confer, the team captain giving the answer for the team. Each team is asked the same number of questions (usually 4, 5 or 6) and is given a set time to answer each one. Questions not answered correctly do *not* go on offer to other teams.

Whilst in some versions equal scores are awarded for each correct answer (usually three points for each) I prefer a more drastic method. One point is awarded to a team for their first correct answer, two points for their second correct answer, three points for their third correct answer and so on. On this basis, a team getting four correct answers in a team round, for example, would score a total of ten points.

4. *The 'Frantic' Quiz*

The reason why this is known as a 'frantic' quiz is because it is fast and furious, exciting for both participants and spectators and is usually over within a few minutes. It is usually a contest between two individuals, often used in pubs who operate it as part of a knockout tournament.

It does, however, suffer from some drawbacks. Buzzers must be used (see Chapter 3: The Buzzer) and the quiz is ruined should these become faulty. Activity tends to become frenetic and both the QM and the scorer must be very sharp.

I have described it here as a contest between two individuals but there is no reason why it could not be adapted for more than two individuals competing against each other, or for teams.

In the opening round, competitors are asked alternate questions but are put under some time pressure to answer. They score a point for each correct answer but should they not be able to answer it correctly their opponent is given the opportunity of answering it for a bonus point. The opening round usually consists of about 6 questions (although there is no reason why this could not be extended) and is really no more than an opportunity for players to 'open their account' and start the second round with a positive balance.

At the end of the first round the scores are read out and the second round commences. A set time is fixed for this round (5 minutes or so, depending on the number of contests expected to take place) and the end of the round marks the end of the contest.

The QM reads out the question and the first person who presses the buzzer is invited to answer. If he answers correctly he scores a point, but if he answers incorrectly or hesitates for too long a point is awarded to his opponent. That question does *not* go on offer: the QM reads out the correct answer and asks the next question. To maintain the flow of the game, should no-one press smartly, then the QM should read out the answer and continue with the next question. Equally, if someone interrupts the question, then the QM should stop reading it out and demand an answer. Contestants failing to begin an answer within a short, agreed time (3–5 seconds) are penalized as if they had answered incorrectly.

5. *'Spotlight Quiz'*
Another quiz format suitable as a contest between individuals which avoids the use of buzzers, is an adaptation of TV's 'Mastermind'. Each contestant is subjected to a set time answering general knowledge questions with the aim of answering as many as possible correctly within that time limit.

The QM directs a series of questions to the contestant who either answers them correctly and is awarded a point, answers them incorrectly and scores no points but has the correct answer read out, or indicates he is not making any attempt to answer and 'passes', in which case no points are awarded and the next question is read out. The answers to any 'passed' questions are read out at the end of the round.

Questions (and answers) need to be of approximately equal length as it is obviously unfair to ask some contestants a string of short questions such as 'What colour are emeralds?' [A – 'Green'], whilst others are asked much longer ones such as 'What is the subtitle to the 1964 film starring Peter Sellers in three roles, as the President of the United States, a British Army Captain and a wheelchair-bound mad inventor?' [A – 'How I Learned to Stop Worrying and Love the Bomb'].

This type of format, just like the 'Frantic Quiz', relies as much on speed as on knowledge and uses up an alarming quantity of questions. When you consider that a quick contestant could use up at least 20 questions in a two minute session, it is vital that you have more than sufficient questions available to ask. It is equally important that the QM reads out the questions clearly, for stopping a watch to repeat a question can destroy the quiz for both the contestant and audience.

3

THE BUZZER

If the quiz format you have chosen involves a round (or rounds) of questions in which speed against other contestants is all-important, some system for deciding who indicated first and thus who should be given the opportunity to answer must be used.

To achieve this the apparatus used should include the following elements:

a) A light, or some sort of indicator which shows the QM who has pressed first and thus who should be asked the question.

b) A buzzer, or some sort of noise which alerts the QM to the fact that someone has switched their light on. Remember that the QM is likely to be looking at the question card and not at the contestants and may not otherwise be aware of a light going on.

c) A system whereby only one light can work at any one time. As soon as the first person activates his light, no other light can go on (you can imagine the difficulties if the QM looked up to find more than one light on!).

d) A method to clear the circuit once a question has been disposed of, so that all lights are switched off and the next question can be asked without disadvantage to any competitor.

e) It must be robust enough to withstand some fairly heavy handling by contestants. Whilst few people would normally switch lights on by hammering on the switch, the same cannot be said of quiz contestants in a panic! Equally, avoid

trailing wires that people may trip over and try to secure
items such as lights to prevent them from being broken.

At an elementary level this can be achieved using a simple
method such as a hotel reception bell-push (the type demonstrated by Dustin Hoffman in the film 'The Graduate') firmly
secured equidistant between two contestants. As long as the
contestants are warned not to remove their hands after
pressing, the QM will be alerted by the sound and can
determine who pressed by seeing whose hand is on the button.

For those who prefer an electrical rather than a mechanical
system the same effect can be achieved by using a single push
button switch to a bell or buzzer (such as a doorbell).

If you prefer something more sophisticated it is certainly
feasible to construct a system along the lines of the circuit
diagram shown below. However, it is not particularly cheap or

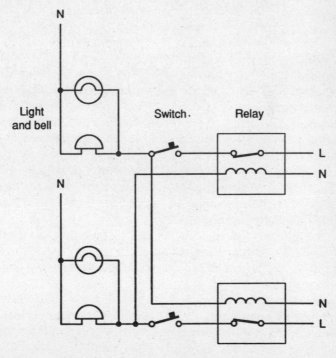

easy to construct and I would advise you to seek the advice of an expert before construction and to check whether the expense is really justified. For safety reasons, *always* run it off batteries and *not* the mains.

Before starting the quiz, explain to the contestants how it operates and get them to test it, so that they – and you – are confident that it is operating satisfactorily.

4
SETTING THE QUESTIONS

Having decided upon a format for the quiz, the final – but no less vital – stage is to set the questions. Far too many compilers rely heavily on obtaining their questions from popular quiz books (which may appear to be a good source), but this suffers from the problem that if the compiler has access to these books, so might the contestants! Indeed, on one occasion I was at a quiz evening where the first thirty questions were taken, verbatim, from a quiz-book I had been browsing through only the day before. Although my team went on to win we did not regard that evening as being particularly enjoyable.

So if you are advised against 'cribbing' questions, just how are you going to compile a set, and from where will you glean your inspiration and information?

One option is to avoid this stage altogether. Some organisations (both commercial and charitable) will provide you with 'specially prepared' sets of questions and answers *but at a price*. This method certainly saves time and effort but suffers from two distinct drawbacks. Firstly, quizzes are usually run on a shoestring budget and such expenses may not always be justified. Secondly, you have to take it on trust that the compiler has correctly gauged what is of interest to, and of the right standard for, a group of people they have never met. After all, would it really be appropriate to ask a round of questions on classical music at a youth club or a round of questions on association football at a local Women's Institute?

Unless you can conscript a friend to compile the questions for you, you are compelled to take on the task yourself. How should you set about this?

Whilst it is inadvisable to use questions from published quiz-books, or from questions asked on radio and television *as they stand*, they can often provide useful pointers as to the *type* of question that can be asked. For example, if you read the question 'What was the name of the dog in Enid Blyton's Famous Five Books?' [A – 'Timmy'], it might lead you to consider asking a different question on the same theme such as 'How many children comprised Enid Blyton's "Famous Five"?' [A – 'Four'] or 'What are Dick, Julian, George, Anne and Timmy known as in children's literature?' [A – 'The Famous Five']. *Adapting* other people's questions is perfectly acceptable – particularly if you can make them more interesting or more appropriate for the format of your quiz.

It is surprising where you can find inspiration when compiling questions, particularly if you become deliberately inquisitive about things around you.

The first set of questions I ever compiled arose largely from being inquisitive about those items with which I came into contact during a normal day. Sitting down for breakfast I was taken by a logo on a cereal packet, which I later used as the basis of a written team question involving identifying various organisations or products from their logos. Whilst reading the morning newspaper I noticed the slogan on the front page and this led to the question 'On the front page of which national daily newspaper would you find the outline of a crusader in red ink?' [A – 'Daily Express'] and I was sufficiently intrigued by seeing a crossword to do some research. That question became 'Which Sunday newspaper, in 1924, was the first British newspaper to publish a crossword?' [A – 'Sunday Express'].

On leaving home I became fascinated by some of the cars that I saw and this led me to come up with the questions 'Which car company manufactures a model called the "Charade"?' [A – 'Daihatsu'] and 'What is the most common colour of cars on British roads?' [A – 'Red']. Having paid to park my car I became interested in my change and quickly had the question

'Where would you be most likely to see the Latin inscription "Decus Et Tutamen"?' [A – 'On an English one pound coin']. By lunchtime I had listed over 30 questions and whilst I later discarded some and had to look up the answers to others, at least I had the start of an entire quiz.

It is always worth consulting good reference works in order both to get ideas for questions and to verify answers to all of your questions. It is less than professional to ask a perfectly valid question only to announce an incorrect answer! If necessary, refer to the source in the question to avoid any complaints from the participants, e.g. 'According to the Encyclopaedia Britannica, who first coined the phrase "Iron Curtain"?' [A – 'Joseph Goebbels'], a useful precaution when many people seem convinced the answer should be Winston Churchill!

Whilst you may well, in time, build up your own store of reference works should you continue to compile quizzes on a fairly frequent basis, most are likely to be stocked in your local public library and although they may be unwilling to lend them to you (because they are so frequently consulted for a few minutes each by a large number of people) you too can call in and consult them on the library premises.

One such book I would thoroughly recommend is Whitaker's Almanack, which is updated each year. By no stretch of the imagination could it be described as a racy read but, being authoritative, well indexed and containing a wealth of useful information, it is an indispensable aid to the quiz compiler. Just reading through its lists of currencies of the world, capital cities or even Parliamentary constituencies can give rise to a wealth of questions.

Your local Reference Librarian can help you by suggesting the standard works on most subjects but for general reference enquiries you may care to consult the 'Shell Book of Firsts', the 'Guinness Book of Answers', the 'Guinness Book of Records' or even a good encyclopaedia or dictionary. However, always ensure that the book you consult is up to date: it is not unlikely that the answer to the question 'What is the world's tallest building?' will change every few years. A reference book that is out of date may well give an incorrect answer.

There are appropriate reference works for virtually all the major topics for quiz questions: 'Halliwell's Film Guide', 'Halliwell's Television Companion', 'Guinness British Hit Singles', for example, are all standard authoritative works which have provided the source of millions of quiz questions across the country. For questions on sport, 'The Guinness Encyclopaedia of Sports Records and Results' or 'The Official World Encyclopaedia of Sports and Games' both cover virtually all sports, whilst Rothmans publish yearbooks on a variety of individual sports. Obviously you will need to go no further than the latest edition of 'Wisden' if you are trying to find something out about cricket. If a question is worth asking, you must be able to find the answer *somewhere*!

The usefulness of newspapers can extend beyond their coverage of current affairs. I have often found good material for questions among the quality Sunday papers, particularly in the book reviews which have often made me raise my eyebrows and think 'I never knew *that*!'

Do not shy away from more solid sources. Encyclopaedias and atlases are always useful – but, as always, ensure that you are consulting an up-to-date edition.

Having written down the ideas for questions it is necessary to ensure that they are fairly balanced and not heavily weighted towards one or two particular areas of knowledge. If the quiz is billed as being 'general knowledge' it would obviously be inappropriate to ask 90% of the questions on the subject of, say, television, just because you used the Radio Times and TV Times as your only sources. Ensure that you ask questions on as wide a range of subjects as possible to ensure that the quiz is not only fair but that the participants regard it as such.

Other than getting ideas on the types of question to be asked, the hardest part of compiling a set of quiz questions is to *phrase* them correctly. The following examples are offered as guidelines to be borne in mind when you have reached this stage. Not all will be appropriate to the type of quiz you are compiling, but some may well prevent arguments or problems at the function itself.

Guidelines for question setting

1. Avoid asking a difficult question first. It is probably only psychological but the confidence of participants is likely to drop sharply if they are unable to answer the very first question.

2. Questions should be answerable – not necessarily by everyone competing, but you should avoid asking questions which are so obscure that it would be a surprise if anyone knew the answer e.g. 'What was the title of the song on the B-side of "I Don't Like Mondays" by The Boomtown Rats?' [A – 'It's all the Rage']. Nor should they be unnecessarily difficult e.g. 'How many metres high is the world's highest mountain?' [A – '8,848 metres'].

3. Be precise in order to avoid confusion. For example, the answer to the question 'Which actor played the part of Hawkeye Pearce in "MASH"?', depends on whether you are referring to the 1970 film version [A – 'Donald Sutherland], or the long-running TV version [A – 'Alan Alda']. Indeed, when referring to films, always identify it by its year of release or the name of its director, as there is often more than one version of the same film: 'Who played Richard Hannay in the film "The Thirty-Nine Steps"?' rather depends to which of the three versions you are referring [A – 'Robert Donat (1935), Kenneth More (1959) or Robert Powell (1978)']. Ensure that each question is clear and unambiguous.

4. Indicate in the phrasing of the questions the type of answer you are seeking. The question 'Where is Mount Everest?' could elicit the replies 'Nepal', 'Asia' or 'the Himalayas' – all equally correct. However, if the question was rephrased 'In which country is the summit of Mount Everest?' only one answer can be counted as correct [A – 'Nepal'].

5. Avoid asking questions which seek answers in the form of an explanation, for these can be difficult to adjudicate! For all of its merits, Radio 4's 'Brain of Britain' suffers from this problem, with Robert Robinson struggling to decide whether a contestant, in answer to the question 'In cricket, what sort of delivery is known as a Chinaman?', has done

enough to earn a point by answering 'a ball which spins from the offside towards the stumps'. Not only would some knowledge of cricket be useful in adjudicating this but a decision will have to be made as to whether the answer, in failing to mention that it is a delivery from a left-handed bowler to a right-handed batsman, is adequate to score a point. This problem could have been avoided by rephrasing the question to read 'In the game of cricket what name is given to an off-break bowled by a left-handed bowler to a right-handed batsman?'.

6. Avoid asking questions which demand more than one answer. It is a matter of judgement whether it is fair to ask a question such as 'Who played the title roles in the 1969 film "Butch Cassidy and the Sundance Kid"?' [A – 'Paul Newman and Robert Redford']. For most questions an answer is either right or it is wrong and a team which can name one of the two actors has failed to answer the question correctly and thus fails to score a mark; yet did they not do better than another team which failed to name cither? If you *do* decide to ask this type of question, emphasise that you must have both answers in order to score, e.g. 'Name *both* the actors . . .'. This problem could have been overcome by rephrasing the question along the lines of 'which actor played the part of the Sundance Kid in the 1969 film "Butch Cassidy and the Sundance Kid"?' [A – 'Robert Redford'].

7. Avoid linking questions in such a way that the answers to subsequent questions depend on knowledge of the first, particularly in written quizzes where the answers to questions are not announced immediately. For example, avoid linking questions such as 'Who was Henry VIII's third wife?' [A – 'Jane Seymour'] followed by 'And which English monarch was their only child?' [A – 'Edward VI']. If a team believes Anne Boleyn was Henry VIII's third wife, then they would probably believe Elizabeth I to be the answer to the second question.

8. Make the questions appropriate for the format of the quiz. If the quiz is a 'quickfire' quiz, particularly when used in

conjunction with a buzzer, they should be of the 'you know it or you don't' variety: 'In which year was the Battle of Trafalgar?' [A – '1805'] is a reasonable example. If a contestant knows the answer it will come to them within a few seconds, but if they do not then it is unlikely that any amount of time will assist them in working out the correct answer.

Whilst it is not always possible to exclude this type of question altogether from a team quiz such as the 'social quiz', it is advisable to design questions such that wherever possible they avoid the prospect of a team sitting around bored because they have answered the question immediately and are waiting for the next one to be read out. Questions which seek a range of knowledge, particularly when it is likely to be supplied by several members of a team acting together, are a useful device. The question 'If you were born on St. Swithin's Day what would be your sign of the zodiac?' [A – 'Cancer'] is a good example. I suspect only a relatively small proportion of individuals could answer this question correctly but for a team event which involves consultation it becomes a rather good question. Providing someone knows the date of St Swithin's Day (15th July) it may well be worked out if someone in the team has a birthday around that time or, if they have not, by eliminating other signs of the zodiac according to the various team-members' own signs. I assume that most people do at least know their own birth sign!

9. If questions 'go on offer' when answered incorrectly, avoid questions with a limited range of plausible (though incorrect!) answers. The question 'Roquefort cheese is made from the milk of which animal?' [A – 'Ewe'] has a limited range of options as very few cheeses are made from anything other than the milk of cows, ewes or goats. If one team selects the wrong answer they have in effect reduced the options for their opponents, who can score a bonus on a 50–50 chance!

10. Be precise, but be concise! For questions that are read out, try to avoid long-winded ones as they tend to impede the

flow of the quiz and are more likely to need repeating, sometimes more than once. Having said this, it is more important that questions are precise but there is often a fine dividing line between being precise and being concise and this is very much down to the discretion of the compiler.

11. Unless you are certain that all the contestants are local, avoid too many questions about the locality. On one occasion I was invited by a publican I knew to a quiz where an entire round of questions was on local pubs. Whilst it may have been a ruse to let the regulars do better, I had never before been within 20 miles of the place and by no means was I the only one.

12. How exact need the answers be? Usually, an answer given by a contestant is either right or it is wrong. No credit is given for a 'near-miss'. For this reason, when compiling questions I have always tended to avoid including those which begin 'in which year did . . .'. Take the question 'In which year was the Battle of Austerlitz fought?' [A – '1805'] and imagine that three teams come up with the answers '1805', '1806' and '1645'. Only the first team would score a point but for the second team, who were only one year out, a miss was as good as a mile and they score no more than the team which placed the event in the wrong century. Fair as far as answering the question is concerned but be aware that although they were incorrect it is likely to rankle with the second team.

If the event being asked about is unlikely to be known that precisely by any of the contestants, you can always widen the net for acceptable correct answers by prefacing questions with 'in which decade did . . .' or by adding words such as ' . . . and we will allow you to be 3 years out, either way'.

13. Avoid asking questions with too many alternative correct answers. Whilst there is nothing wrong in asking questions where an alternative answer is acceptable, such as 'According to the Collins English Dictionary, which organisation is denoted with the letters RSC?' [A – 'Royal Shakespeare Company *or* Royal Society of Chemistry'] it is significantly

harder to mark where the possible number of correct answers reaches double figures or more. For example, it would be difficult enough in a written team quiz to mark a question such as 'Name a landlocked country' as you would have to compare answers with a long list of such countries; it would completely ruin the tempo of a frantic quiz with the QM desperately scanning through the possible answers to check whether an answer was correct or not.

When compiling a quiz a perennial problem is trying to pitch the questions at the right level. If too many of the questions cannot be answered by the majority of the participants then they are likely to be put off and are less likely to enjoy the experience. If most of the participants know most of the answers then it is less of a contest. The problem is trying to gauge the overall breadth of knowledge of participants in advance such that a happy balance of questions is posed but there is no easy way to this!

There is no adequate definition of a 'hard' question or an 'easy' question and indeed there is much truth in the pat response that an 'easy' question is one to which you know the correct answer. Certainly it becomes easier to gauge with experience but still not with any certainty. I have posed the same set of questions at two team quizzes at venues many miles apart on successive evenings and was surprised to find that the winning score of the first evening would have been insufficient to have placed that team in the first ten on the second evening.

This might be explained by the types of people involved each time (certainly, on the second evening there were a number of people participating who were avid attenders of quizzes) or possibly because the range of questions was more suited to their interests. When compiling quizzes, keep in mind the type of person likely to attend.

It is always possible to try out a set of questions on a (non-participating!) friend in advance but this has limited advantages. It may help you with your pronunciation or to iron out any problems with phrasing but you cannot infer that, because your friend knew virtually all (or none) of the answers, the participants will do likewise. The problem is to find a friend who can act as a reliable benchmark.

When compiling quizzes for a 'social quiz' I try to ensure that in each of the rounds half of the questions will be answered correctly by all the teams, that two or three questions will be answered by half of the teams, whilst the rest will only be answered by one or two teams. I have to admit that I do not succeed very often: invariably I over-estimate (or under-estimate) their breadth of knowledge, though now I rarely find that a team fails to score anything in a round (which I am sure they find even more embarrassing than I do).

My advice is that when you have compiled a set of questions, read through them and replace some if it appears that the overall standard is either too high or too low for the participants. This is a subjective exercise; though experience will help, it will not make it an exact science. You know which questions you would have been able to answer, but you can never know in advance which questions other people will be able to answer correctly.

5

SAMPLE QUESTIONS

The following questions are included to assist you with compiling your own set by not only showing you the range of topics that can be broached but also the way in which questions should be phrased.

They were intended for varying standards of contestants and have all been used at quizzes with different formats. The first questions, which are all in groups of 10, are more suitable for the type of quiz where time is allowed for consideration and conferring (such as the 'social quiz', the 'team quiz' and the 'pub quiz'). The 'quick questions' which start on page 100 are exactly that – questions which contestants either know the answer to or do not – and are designed to be asked, and answered, swiftly. This makes them more suitable for the 'frantic quiz' or the 'spotlight quiz' between individuals.

At the end, starting on page 139, I have included some typical 'gamble questions' and, on page 143, 'written team questions' that I have used in the 'social quiz'. The answers start on page 156.

General Knowledge 1 (*Answers on page 156*)
1. Where would you be most likely to see the Latin inscription 'Decus et Tutamen'?
2. How much does Park Lane cost to buy on a Monopoly board?
3. Which annual British sporting event takes place over a course 4 miles 374 yards long?
4. Which country was known to the Romans as Hibernia?

5. Sculpted by Frederic Auguste Bartholdi, which statue was dedicated in 1886 on Bedloe's Island?
6. Name either U.S. state whose shape is a rectangle.
7. Which is the only letter of the alphabet which you will not find in the names of any of the states of the USA?
8. What is the fifth letter of the Greek alphabet?
9. What would be collected by an arctophilist?
10. If the books of the Bible were arranged in alphabetical order, which book would come last?

General Knowledge 2 (*Answers on page 156*)
1. Which battle of 1066 shares its name with a football league ground?
2. Who lives at No. 12 Downing Street?
3. How many squares are there on a Scrabble board?
4. By what name do we know Rodrigo Diaz del Bivar?
5. Which three colours make up the French flag?
6. What is added to gin to make it 'pink'?
7. How is 500 represented in Roman numerals?
8. Excluding the cue ball, how many balls are there on the table at the start of a game of snooker?
9. Which English county has the longest coastline?
10. What letter comes next in this sequence:–
    M   V   E   M   J   S   U   N   ?

General Knowledge 3 (*Answers on page 156*)
1. What was invented by Doctor Ludwig Zamenhoff in 1887?
2. How many bottles of champagne are contained in a Jeroboam?
3. What is collected by a deltiologist?
4. If you were born on St. Stephen's Day, what would be your sign of the zodiac?
5. The ancient city of Carthage was situated in the territory of which modern country?
6. In heraldry, what colour is described as 'gules'?
7. Which car company is known for the model called the 'Charade'?
8. What is the value of the letter 'K' in Scrabble?

9.   How many dominoes make up a set?
10.   If five equals wood and ten equals tin, what does twenty-five equal?

General Knowledge 4 (*Answers on page 156*)
1.   The national anthem of which European country has no words?
2.   What is otalgia?
3.   Which character in fiction wrote a monograph on the ashes of 140 different varieties of tobacco?
4.   What is the common name for the illness known as pertussis?
5.   What do Margaret Kempson and Margaret Roberts have in common (other than sharing the same Christian name!)?
6.   How many different opening moves does white have the choice from (other than resigning!) at the start of a game of chess?
7.   Which invention – made of bicycle parts, lenses, cocoa tins, sealing wax and string – was first successfully demonstrated on 26 January 1926?
8.   What would be collected by a phillumenist?
9.   Who was Governor and Commander-in-Chief of the Bahamas from 1940 to 1945?
10.   Which alcoholic drink was first made by a French monk from Hautvilliers?

General Knowledge 5 (*Answers on page 156*)
1.   What is studied by a vexillologist?
2.   In the Royal Navy, how many bells are sounded at the end of a dog watch?
3.   What name is given to the iron plates which hold the rails together on a railway track?
4.   Who was the first British monarch to be born in the twentieth century?
5.   If a piece of silver was hallmarked with an anchor, from which British city would it have come?
6.   Which country's postage stamps bear the inscription 'Suomi'?

7. How many years were there between the Silver Jubilees of George V and Elizabeth II?
8. Which Sunday newspaper, in 1924, published the first crossword to appear in a British newspaper?
9. Which English town did the Romans call 'Eboracum'?
10. On a standard English Monopoly board, which is the only property you can build houses on south of the River Thames?

General Knowledge 6 (*Answers on page 157*)

1. Who was the first Roman Catholic to be elected U.S. President?
2. Who wrote the 'General Theory of Employment, Interest, and Money' in 1936?
3. What colour is a female blackbird?
4. On a standard map of the London underground, what colour is the Bakerloo line?
5. Name the first Englishwoman to hold the office of Mayor, as well as being one of the first women to enter the medical profession.
6. What is the last book of the Old Testament?
7. Who was the second man to walk on the moon?
8. Which military leader came fifth in the Modern Pentathlon at the 1924 Olympic Games?
9. Name the capital of Nova Scotia.
10. Which letter comes next in this sequence:–
    Z   X   C   V   B   N   ?

General Knowledge 7 (*Answers on page 157*)

1. How many millimetres in a kilometre?
2. Which youth organisation was founded by William A. Smith in Glasgow in 1883?
3. Which is the middle letter on the middle line on a standard typewriter keyboard?
4. If something was described as 'dodecagonal', how many sides would it have?
5. With what activity is a campanologist concerned?
6. In a rainbow, which colour lies between yellow and red?

7.   How many pieces does each player have at the start of a game of backgammon?
8.   Who was leader of the Liberal Party when Margaret Thatcher became leader of the Conservative Party?
9.   Which category of Nobel Prize was first awarded in 1969?
10.   Which South American city is the highest capital city in the world?

General Knowledge 8 (*Answers on page 157*)
1.   What proportion of the total votes cast in a constituency must a candidate obtain to receive a refund of their deposit in a British parliamentary election?
2.   In human anatomy, what is the 'hallux'?
3.   Who was the trainer of the steeplechaser Desert Orchid?
4.   The French call it 'La Manche'. What is it known as in Britain?
5.   What is the surname of Roy of the Rovers?
6.   How many pounds does one gallon of water weigh?
7.   Where did Moses receive the Ten Commandments?
8.   Other than being famous historical characters, what in particular have St. Paul, Raleigh, Montgomery and Bismarck in common?
9.   Which are the only two words to appear on the George Cross?
10.   Which of the following years are *not* leap years:–
      1900, 1920, 1940, 1960, 1980, 2000?

General Knowledge 9 (*Answers on page 157*)
1.   If you were celebrating your China Wedding anniversary, for how many years would you have been married?
2.   On which mountain in South Dakota would you find carvings of the faces of Washington, Lincoln, Jefferson and Roosevelt?
3.   In the grounds of which building is the annual Chelsea Flower Show held each May?
4.   In golf, what distinguishes a links course from other golf courses?
5.   In which U.S. state would you find Fort Knox?

6.   Which twentieth century British Prime Minister shares the same name as the nineteenth century Colonel who first concocted the game of snooker?
7.   What colour lies between green and indigo in a rainbow?
8.   Which chicken dish was named after a battle of 1800?
9.   Who was awarded the 1961 Nobel Peace Prize post-humously?
10.   Which peers of the realm rank between Earls and Dukes?

General Knowledge 10 (*Answers on page 157*)
1.   The 17.3 mile tunnel from East Finchley to Morden, the longest on the London Underground system, is on which line?
2.   How many different opening moves does black have the choice from at the start of a game of draughts?
3.   What comes next in the sequence: green, amber, red?
4.   Which sign of the zodiac is not an animal?
5.   What term in ballet is given to a complete turn on one leg, performed either on the ball of the foot or on the toes?
6.   In a standard domestic plug, what colour is the earth wire?
7.   The badge of which organisation consists of a red cross and an anchor with the words 'Sure and Stedfast' on it?
8.   In which town is the University of Ulster based?
9.   At the start of a game of draughts, how many squares on the board are not covered by pieces?
10.   What is the total of the seven Roman numerals?

General Knowledge 11 (*Answers on page 157*)
1.   Alongside which river is Balmoral Castle?
2.   What nationality was the first Secretary-General of the United Nations?
3.   What do the following women have in common: Sally Ride, Helen Sharman and Svetlana Savitskaya?
4.   Which English county was known to the Romans as Vectis?
5.   Which colour is associated with a government document intended to stimulate discussion prior to the government

coming to its own conclusions?

6. Which European country has the oldest Parliament?
7. For what did the acronym E.N.S.A. stand?
8. Who was the first Archbishop of Canterbury?
9. In which British newspaper are the adventures of Rupert Bear featured?
10. Also remembered for introducing the pillar box, who wrote the 'Barsetshire' novels?

General Knowledge 12 (*Answers on page 158*)

1. Which country has the international car registration letter 'L'?
2. He lived from 1624 to 1691 and founded the Quaker movement, the Society of Friends. Who was he?
3. Which English cathedral has famous stained glass windows called 'The Five Sisters', and an East window which is one of the largest stained glass windows in the world?
4. What is always taken to the F.A. Cup Final, but never used?
5. Which famous university was founded in 1636 at Cambridge, Massachusetts?
6. What colour is the Circle Line on a London Underground map?
7. Which term has been coined to describe 19th October, 1987?
8. What name is given to the tenth day of Tishri?
9. In which U.S. city was the 1964 Nobel Peace Prize winner assassinated?
10. In 1945, what was 15th August in the UK, but 2nd September in the USA?

General Knowledge 13 (*Answers on page 158*)

1. Who was the first woman to win a Nobel Prize?
2. Of which European country is St. Denis the patron saint?
3. Where are the Descartes Highlands, first scaled by Captain John Watts Young of the United States Navy in April 1972?
4. What was designed by Sir Joseph Paxton for the 1851

Great Exhibition, moved to Sydenham in 1854, and was destroyed by fire in 1936?

5. What is the equivalent rank in the R.A.F. to that of Vice-Admiral in the Navy?

6. In Asia, which religion has the most adherents?

7. Which famous aviator disappeared in 1937 after taking off from New Guinea whilst attempting to fly around the equator?

8. Which famous Wild West character was shot and killed by Bob Ford?

9. What was the name of Captain Fitzroy's ship that sailed around the world from December 1831 to October 1836, and provided the inspiration for a famous book published over 20 years later?

10. In which sport or game are the phrases 'j'adoube' and 'en passant' used?

General Knowledge 14 (*Answers on page 158*)

1. What ceased to be legal tender in the UK on 21st November 1970?

2. Which number is diametrically opposite the twenty on a dartboard?

3. Which organisation formed the subject matter of the 1968 Fulton Report?

4. Which company was the first to issue travellers' cheques in their current form?

5. Which invention was first demonstrated using an empty food can (open at one end), a Lyons coffee tin (with both ends removed), a vacuum cleaner and a set of kitchen scales?

6. Who was the first English actor to be knighted for his services to the theatre?

7. How many species of snake are native to Ireland?

8. Which is the largest internal organ in the human body?

9. In which institution would you find the Lutine Bell?

10. Which collective noun describes a group of owls?

General Knowledge 15 (*Answers on page 158*)

1. What was the name of the last steam locomotive to be built by British Rail?
2. Which British newspaper went tabloid on 3rd May 1971?
3. By what name is the plant 'saintpaulia' better known?
4. Which British bird has the most feathers?
5. In which modern country would you find the site of the Hanging Gardens of Babylon?
6. Which famous building would you find at 1600 Pennsylvania Avenue?
7. How many stars make up the constellation known as the Plough?
8. Who said, in 1973, 'Some people think football is a matter of life and death. I don't like that attitude. I can assure them it is much more serious than that'?
9. How is ten expressed in binary?
10. What was designed by Harry Beck and first published in 1933, and although subjected to necessary modernisation, exists in a substantially similar format today?

General Knowledge 16 (*Answers on page 158*)

1. Which number comes next in this sequence:–
    20   1   18   4   13   6   ?
2. What was invented by Gottlieb Daimler in 1885, first raced over a one mile course at Richmond, Surrey in 1897, and now races under the auspices of the governing body the F.I.M.?
3. Which is the most common word in spoken English?
4. Which London theatre opened its doors for the first time in 1818 as 'The Royal Coburg'?
5. Which car manufacturer had models called the 'Fuego' and the 'Dauphine'?
6. Who, in Arthurian legend, threw Excalibur into the lake?
7. Who created the cartoon character 'Colonel Blimp'?
8. How many years after your silver wedding would you celebrate your diamond wedding?
9. Which city was largely designed by Pierre Charles L'Enfant, became the national seat of government in 1800, although

partially destroyed by British forces in the early part of the nineteenth century?

10. Until 1927, in which city did the Commonwealth Parliament of Australia meet?

General Knowledge 17 (*Answers on page 158*)

1. How many letters of the alphabet can be transmitted in semaphore using only one flag?
2. What was the nationality of the first non-American and non-Russian to go into space in 1978?
3. If you were suffering from anosmia, which of your senses would you have lost?
4. How many points are awarded for an away win on the football pools 'treble chance'?
5. How many people walked on the moon between 1965 and 1985?
6. Asteroids move around the sun primarily between the orbit of Mars and which other planet?
7. What is the points value of the letter 'J' in Scrabble?
8. To the nearest square inch, what would be the area of a circle with a radius of 7 inches?
9. In a standard eleven-a-side game of cricket, what is the maximum number of people allowed on the pitch at any time during play?
10. How many bishops and archbishops of the Church of England are entitled to sit in the House of Lords?

General Knowledge 18 (Connections) (*Answers on page 159*)

1. What did France and Spain do in 1582, Scotland in 1600, Denmark in 1700, but England, Wales and Ireland not do until 1752?
2. What is five feet six inches in Spain, three feet six inches in South Africa, but only four feet eight and a half inches in Britain?
3. Britain had 630 in 1955, 635 in 1974, 650 in 1983 and 651 in 1992. What are they?
4. What did Britain and France do in 1920, Germany in 1926, Russia in 1934 that the U.S.A. never did?

5. What comes next in this sequence:–
    Maurice, Alexander, James, Edward, James, Leonard?
6. What do the following European countries have in common (other than being in Europe!):
    France, Iceland, Luxembourg, Netherlands, Norway, United Kingdom?
7. What do the following countries have in common:–
    Paraguay, Bolivia, Austria, Switzerland, Laos, Afghanistan, Mongolia, Chad, Mali, Niger, Uganda, Zimbabwe?
8. Which city lies at the northern end of the A1?
9. What have Hannibal, Octavius, Moses, Attila, Caractacus and Dante in common?
10. In Britain, what was 92.5% until 1919, 50% until 1946, but 0% thereafter?

Acronyms (*Answers on page 159*)
For what do the following initials stand?
1. OPEC
2. PDSA
3. SEATO
4. SALT
5. NAAFI
6. ERNIE
7. ACAS
8. UNESCO
9. SCUBA
10. MORI

Aliases 1 (*Answers on page 159*)
By what names are the following people better known?
1. Shirley Crabtree
2. Mary Ann Evans
3. Archibald Leach
4. William Pratt
5. George O'Dowd
6. Maurice Micklewight
7. Reginald Dwight
8. Lev Bronstein

9.   Frederick Austerlitz
10.   Norma Jean Baker

Aliases 2 (*Answers on page 159*)
By what names are the following people better known?
1.   Frances Gumm
2.   Cherilyn Sarkasian LaPier
3.   Greta Gustafson
4.   Marjorie Robertson
5.   Robert Zimmerman
6.   Lesley Hornby
7.   Gordon Matthew Sumner
8.   Harry Roger Webb
9.   Arnold George Dorsey
10.   Edson Arantes Do Nascimento

Aliases 3 (*Answers on page 159*)
By what names are the following people better known?
1.   Marion Morrison
2.   Larushka Mischa Skikne
3.   Reverend Charles Lutwidge Dodgson
4.   William Joyce
5.   David Robert Hayward-Jones
6.   Allen Stewart Konigsberg
7.   Eric Arthur Blair
8.   Gertrud Margarete Zelle
9.   David John Moore Cornwell
10.   Domenikos Theotocopoulos

Art 1 (*Answers on page 159*)
1.   In which European city would you find the famous museum and art gallery called the Hermitage?
2.   What was the name of the gallery opened at the Tate in 1987 to house the collection of Joseph Turner's works that he had left to the nation?
3.   What name was adopted in 1848 by a group of artists including Millais, Holman Hunt and Rossetti in response to what they felt was the sorry state of British art?

4.   What name is given to a painting on a wet plastered wall using watercolours?

5.   Which artist was portrayed by Charlton Heston in the 1965 film 'The Agony and the Ecstasy'?

6.   Founded in 1818, in which European city would you find the Prado Museum?

7.   On which Greek island was the painter and sculptor known as El Greco born?

8.   Which French Post-Impressionist painter was once a successful stockbroker?

9.   What was the title of a series of engravings by Hogarth which inspired Stravinsky to write an opera with the same title?

10. Which institution houses the Elgin Marbles?

Art 2 (*Answers on page 160*)

1.   In which city would you find the Uffizi art gallery?

2.   What was the first name of the Florentine artist and sculptor, Buonarroti?

3.   Which single word describes a picture in three parts made such that the two pictures on the side can fold over and hinge above the middle picture?

4.   What colour eyes does the Mona Lisa have?

5.   Who designed the tapestry 'Christ in Glory' to be found at Coventry Cathedral?

6.   Named after one of his works, on which artist's life was the 1974 film 'A Bigger Splash' based?

7.   Which artist was once the manager of the rock group, the Velvet Underground?

8.   Which museum, originally called the Museum of Ornamental Art, was opened in 1857?

9.   Which French artist painted the picture 'Impression: Sunrise' that gave rise to the term 'impressionist'?

10. Which English artist published his own book 'The Anatomy of the Horse' in 1766?

Assassinations (*Answers on page 160*)

1.   In which European city did Gavrilo Princip make a successful assassination attempt on 28th June 1914?

2.   In which American city did Mark Chapman assassinate John Lennon?
3.   Which French revolutionary leader was assassinated by Charlotte Corday?
4.   In Shakespeare, which of the conspirators was the first to stab Julius Caesar?
5.   Which South African President was assassinated on 6th September 1966?
6.   In which year were both Martin Luther King and Robert Kennedy assassinated?
7.   Which political leader was assassinated in October 1984 and was succeeded by her son?
8.   Theodore Roosevelt became U.S. President in 1901 after which President's assassination?
9.   In which American city was Abraham Lincoln assassinated by John Wilkes Booth in 1865?
10. In which country was Lev Bronstein assassinated in July 1940?

The Bible (*Answers on page 160*)
1.   According to Genesis 7, how many humans were in Noah's Ark during the flood?
2.   The Ten Commandments are listed in Exodus and which other book of the Bible?
3.   Which is the shortest book in the Old Testament?
4.   Which of the twelve disciples was Simon Peter's brother?
5.   Who was the father of King Solomon?
6.   On which day did God create man?
7.   What is the sixth book of the New Testament?
8.   Who was Adam and Eve's youngest son?
9.   What nationality was Samson's wife?
10. By what name are the first five books of the Bible collectively known?

Birds 1 (*Answers on page 160*)
1.   What is the alternative name of the Shakespearian character, Robin Goodfellow?
2.   What type of bird appeared in the title of a book by Jack

Higgins, later made into a film starring Michael Caine and Donald Sutherland?

3.   In golf, how many strokes under par is a 'birdie'?

4.   What type of bird did William Wordsworth address with the words 'Shall I call thee bird, or but a wandering voice'?

5.   Which instrument was played by the jazz musician, Charlie 'Bird' Parker?

6.   Who wrote the story on which the 1963 Alfred Hitchcock film 'The Birds' was based?

7.   Which bird was the title of a 1968 UK number one hit single by Fleetwood Mac?

8.   In the famous Monty Python's 'parrot sketch', what breed of parrot had John Cleese supposedly been sold?

9.   Which English football league team are nicknamed the 'Eagles'?

10.   Which high street bank uses the eagle as its logo?

Birds 2 (*Answers on page 160*)

1.   Which type of bird might be garganeys, gadwalls, pintails or goosanders?

2.   What is the alternative English name for the Hedge Sparrow?

3.   Which is the heaviest breed of bird still surviving today?

4.   Which collective noun describes a group of crows?

5.   Which type of birds are especially associated with the Tower of London?

6.   Which British breed of bird always lays its eggs in the nests of other birds?

7.   Which is the only breed of bird that can fly backwards?

8.   Although becoming extinct about 200 years ago, in which country were moa last recorded?

9.   Which tiny brown-barred British bird has the scientific name 'troglodytes troglodytes'?

10.   In which country are budgerigars found in the wild?

Books and Films (*Answers on page 160*)

1.   Which book by P.C. Wren, was made into a silent film in 1926, re-made in 1939 starring Ray Milland and Gary

Cooper, and re-made yet again in 1966 starring Telly Savalas and Doug McClure?

2. Which novel by A.E.W. Mason set in the Sudan and telling the story of an Englishman eager to prove that he is not a coward, has been filmed several times, including a 1939 version starring Ralph Richardson, and a 1977 TV movie starring Beau Bridges, Jane Seymour, Robert Powell and Simon Ward?

3. Which 1939 film was based on a story by L. Frank Baum?

4. Who wrote the novel on which the 1961 film 'The Guns of Navarone' was based?

5. Which 1975 film starring Jack Nicholson was based on a novel by Ken Kesey?

6. Which 1964 Walt Disney film was based on a book by P.L. Travers?

7. Which 1968 film directed by Stanley Kubrick was based on the story 'The Sentinel' written by Arthur C. Clarke?

8. Which 1939 film, directed by Victor Fleming, was based on the only novel ever written by Margaret Mitchell?

9. Which writer wrote the book on which the 1980 film 'The Shining' was based?

10. Who wrote the book on which the film 'Chitty Chitty Bang Bang' was based?

City and Finance (*Answers on page 161*)

1. In the City, what do the letters U.S.M. stand for?

2. What is measured on the Hang Seng Index?

3. In the financial world which term, also the name of an animal, is applied to a person who intends to make a profit on buying new share issues and selling them as soon as dealings start?

4. In which thoroughfare is the Bank of England situated?

5. What position has been held by L.K. O'Brien, D.H.F. Somerset and G.M. Gill?

6. What does the acronym M.I.R.A.S. stand for?

7. Centred round the activities of a British company which sought to take over responsibility for the National Debt in return for a monopoly of trade with South America, what

name is given to the financial crash of 1720 which resulted
in the imprisonment of the Chancellor of the Exchequer?
8. How many shares comprise the Financial Times Industrial
Ordinary Share Index?
9. In which city is Italy's main Stock Exchange?
10. What does the acronym 'PEP' stand for?

Coins and Medals (*Answers on page 161*)
1. In pre-decimal coinage, how many groats equalled a
guinea?
2. On which current British coin would you find the Prince of
Wales' feathers?
3. How many sides did the pre-decimal British threepence
have around its edge?
4. After 1937, which British bird was featured on a farthing?
5. What inscription does the Victoria Cross have on it?
6. Which weighs most: 500 one pence coins or 250 twopence
coins?
7. What event was commemorated on the 1965 British
crown?
8. Which event of the late 1940's led to a change in the
wording which appeared on British coinage?
9. What is the United States of America's highest military
decoration?
10. Other than building, in what trade or profession might
'quoins' be used?

Currencies (*Answers on page 161*)
What is the main unit of currency of the following
countries:–
1. Finland
2. Australia
3. Kenya
4. Pakistan
5. Tunisia
6. Zimbabwe
7. Saudi Arabia
8. Morocco

9.   Cuba
10.   People's Republic of China

Famous Animals (*Answers on page 161*)

1.   What was the name of Tonto's horse in the 'Lone
      Ranger'?
2.   What was the name of the dog that found the World Cup
      after it had been stolen in 1966?
3.   In 'The Wizard of Oz', what was the name of Dorothy's
      little dog?
4.   In the series of 'Tarzan' films, what was the name of his
      chimpanzee?
5.   What sort of animals were Chi-Chi and An-An?
6.   What was the name of the dog that used to appear on
      HMV record labels?
7.   Who wrote the novel 'The Plague Dogs', made into an
      animated film in 1982?
8.   What type of animal was Laika, the first living creature to
      be sent into space on Sputnik II in 1957?
9.   In Dickens' 'Oliver Twist', what was the name of Bill
      Sikes' dog?
10.   What type of animal was Baloo in Rudyard Kipling's 'The
      Jungle Book'?

Films 1 (*Answers on page 161*)

1.   Which 1987 film, directed by Steven Spielberg, was
      adapted from an autobiographical novel by J.G. Ballard?
2.   What was the title of the 1980 film, starring John Hurt,
      based on the true story of John Merrick?
3.   What was the title of the 1962 film, starring Karl Malden
      and Burt Lancaster, based on the adventures of Robert
      Stroud?
4.   The 1956 film 'Lust For Life', starring Kirk Douglas and
      Anthony Quinn, was based on the biography of which
      famous artist?
5.   Which 1989 film starring John Hurt and Joanne Whalley-
      Kilmer was based around the Profumo Affair?

6. The 1958 film 'The Inn of the Sixth Happiness', starring Curt Jurgens and Ingrid Bergman, was based on the true story of which British missionary?

7. Portrayed in the film 'Chariots of Fire', in which city were the 1924 Olympics held?

8. Name both the actors who played the parts of the reporters Woodward and Bernstein in the film 'All the President's Men'.

9. Which actor played the title role in the 1954 film 'The Glenn Miller Story'?

10. Which comedian played the part of his own father in a film loosely based on his own wartime experiences?

Films 2 (*Answers on page 161*)

1. Name the film which marked the last screen performance of both Marilyn Monroe and Clark Gable.

2. What was the title of the 1976 musical film based on the story of Cinderella?

3. Which actor played the part of King Henry II in both 'Becket' in 1964, and 'The Lion in Winter' in 1968?

4. Which Spanish artist contributed a dream sequence to the 1945 Alfred Hitchcock film 'Spellbound'?

5. Which 1944 film was centred on the activities of a horse called 'The Pi'?

6. For which film did George C. Scott refuse to accept a best actor Oscar?

7. Which was the first of the 'Carry On' series of films?

8. Which film studio's trademark is a mountain circled by stars?

9. In which 1965 film did Alec Guinness play the part of Omar Sharif's half-brother?

10. Which country provides the setting for the 1974 film 'The Cars That Ate Paris'?

Films 3 (*Answers on page 162*)

1. Which 1953 film starring Richard Burton, Jean Simmons, Victor Mature and Michael Rennie was the first to be shot in cinemascope?

2.   Which 1983 film starring Lee Marvin and William Hurt was based on a novel by Martin Cruz Smith?

3.   Which war formed the setting for the 1978 film 'Go Tell The Spartans', which starred Burt Lancaster?

4.   Which film was the first full-length Walt Disney cartoon?

5.   Which character has been played in films by, amongst others, Errol Flynn, Sean Connery and John Cleese?

6.   Which fictional character has appeared in the most films?

7.   James Dean was originally lined up to play the part of Billy the Kid in the film 'The Left Handed Gun', and the boxer Rocky Grazziano in the film 'Somebody Up There Likes Me', but after his death in 1955 who actually played these parts?

8.   By what name is the 1980's Oscar-winning actor Krishna Banji better known?

9.   Name the film star who wrote his own epitaph: 'On the whole, I'd rather be in Philadelphia.'

10. What was the only film in which both John Wayne and Shirley Temple appeared?

Films 4 – Blue Movies (*Answers on page 162*)

1.   Who sang 'Falling In Love Again' in the 1930 film 'The Blue Angel'?

2.   Who played the part of the Headmistress in the film 'Blue Murder at St. Trinians'?

3.   Which actress played the part of Elvis Presley's mother in the film 'Blue Hawaii', and later went on to play a TV detective?

4.   In which war was 'The Blue Max' set?

5.   Remade in 1980 starring Christopher Atkins and Brooke Shields, who played the female lead in the original 1949 version of 'The Blue Lagoon'?

6.   Who sang the title song to the 1970 film 'Soldier Blue'?

7.   What was the title of the 1988 film, written by Neil Simon, and loosely based on his experiences of ten weeks army training in Missouri towards the end of World War Two?

8.   What was the method of transport featured in the 1986 film 'Blue Thunder'?

9.   Which actor starred alongside John Belushi in the 1980 film 'The Blues Brothers'?

10. The inspiration for the long running TV series 'Dixon of Dock Green' was the 1950 film 'The Blue Lamp', but which actor shot Jack Warner in that film?

Film Directors (*Answers on page 162*)

Who directed the following films:–

1.   Battleship Potemkin (1925)
2.   Brief Encounter (1945)
3.   The Third Man (1949)
4.   Casablanca (1942)
5.   The Godfather (1972)
6.   Heaven's Gate (1980)
7.   Three Men And A Baby (1987)
8.   The Producers (1968)
9.   Walkabout (1971)
10. The Effect of Gamma Rays on Man-in-the-Moon Marigolds (1972)

Film Sequels (*Answers on page 162*)

1.   Which character was played by Claude Rains in 1933, and by Vincent Price in the 1939 sequel?

2.   What was the full title of the film 'Star Trek II'?

3.   Who starred alongside Paul Newman as his protégé in the 1986 sequel to 'The Hustler'?

4.   Which was the first film sequel to have won an Oscar for Best Picture?

5.   What was the title of the 1975 sequel to the film 'That'll Be The Day', both starring David Essex?

6.   'Oliver's Story' was a sequel to which successful 1970 film?

7.   Who replaced Michael Caine in the 1975 film 'Alfie Darling', the sequel to the 1966 'Alfie'?

8.   What was the title of the sequel to the 1974 film 'The Three Musketeers', directed by Richard Lester?

9.   A sequel to which 1960 Alfred Hitchcock film, starring the original leading actor, was made over 20 years later?

10. What was the name of the character played by John

Wayne in the film 'True Grit', which later became the title of its sequel?

Film Title Roles 1 (*Answers on page 162*)

Name the actor or actress who played the title role in the following films:–

1. Lawrence of Arabia (1962)
2. Batman (1989)
3. Dr. No (1962)
4. Brubaker (1980)
5. The Great Dictator (1940)
6. Serpico (1973)
7. The Man Who Fell To Earth (1976)
8. The Admirable Crichton (1957)
9. Barbarella (1968)
10. The Wizard of Oz (1939)

Film Title Roles 2 (*Answers on page 162*)

Name the actor or actress who played the title role in the following films:–

1. The Man With The Golden Arm (1955)
2. Get Carter (1971)
3. Cleopatra (1963)
4. Mr. Hulot's Holiday (1953)
5. Doctor At Large (1957)
6. Dracula (1931)
7. Captain Blood (1935)
8. The Elephant Man (1980)
9. Isadora (1969)
10. She (1965)

Firsts (*Answers on page 162*)

1. Which mountain was first successfully climbed by the Englishman, Edward Whymper, in 1865?
2. Which country won football's first World Cup in 1930?
3. What 'first' was achieved by Valentina Tereshkova on 16 June 1963?
4. What was Louis Washkansky the first to receive, on

December 3rd, 1967?

5.   In which city was the first sub-four minute mile run?

6.   Which U.S. state, the capital of which is Dover, was the first to be admitted to the Union in 1787 and is still known by the appropriate nickname 'The First State'?

7.   Who was first to achieve ten UK number one hit singles?

8.   Built in 1903, which Hertfordshire town was Britain's first 'Garden City'?

9.   Who was the first person successfully to lead an expedition to the North Pole?

10. What were first put on sale in Britain on 6th May 1840, but are now on sale in every country?

Food and Drink 1 (*Answers on page 163*)

1.   Name *both* major ingredients of the dish 'Devils on Horseback'.

2.   Which dessert was created to honour a famous ballerina?

3.   Which spirit forms the base of a Tom Collins cocktail?

4.   In which city did Sally Lunn sell the tea-cakes that bear her name?

5.   What is added to eggs to make them 'eggs florentine'?

6.   Which country produces the wine 'vinho verde'?

7.   By what name is the love apple now better known?

8.   How many gallons are there in a firkin?

9.   Which vegetable is the major ingredient of bortsch?

10. From which country does tabasco sauce originate?

Food and Drink 2 (*Answers on page 163*)

1.   Which vegetable forms the base of sauerkraut?

2.   Which vegetable is known as zucchini in the USA?

3.   Which country produces a semi-hard white cheese called Limburger?

4.   What ingredient is added to wine to make port?

5.   With what is the fish garnished in sole veronique?

6.   Name the brewing company featured in Coronation Street's Rovers Return.

7.   A magnum of champagne is equivalent to how many standard bottles?

8. Which cocktail includes white rum, pineapple juice and coconut?
9. What do the letters V.S.O.P. stand for on a bottle of brandy?
10. If a recipe suggested baking at 150 Centigrade or 300 Fahrenheit, what number should you use if you had a gas oven?

Food and Drink 3 (*Answers on page 163*)
1. What spirit is made by fermenting and distilling the juice of the blue agave plant?
2. In which English city would you find Colman's Mustard Shop and Museum?
3. Which spice is obtained from crocuses?
4. Which fruit is a cross between a peach and a plum?
5. Equal to 37.5 gallons, a *cran* is a unit of capacity used for measuring which type of fish?
6. Under the EC system of grading eggs by weight, how many different grades are there?
7. From the milk of which animal was Mozzarella cheese originally made?
8. What colour top does a bottle of Channel Island milk have?
9. Profiteroles and éclairs are made from which type of pastry?
10. If two Methuselahs equal one Balthazar, what do five Jeroboams equal?

Football (*Answers on page 163*)
1. Which footballer scored for the winning team in each of the first five European Cup Finals?
2. In 1984, which Liverpool Football Club player became the first Briton to be presented with the Adidas Golden Boot Award?
3. Who was the first player to win 100 caps for Scotland?
4. For which team did Jimmy Greaves score a goal in the 1958 Inter-Cities Fairs Cup Final?
5. In 1966, who was the first footballer to win the BBC

Sports Personality of the Year Award?
6. Who has scored a goal in the Final of two World Cups, separated by 12 years?
7. Which football club supplied most players for the England squad at the 1990 World Cup in Italy?
8. Which FA Cup-winning side is the only team to have been champions of all four divisions and Division 3 North?
9. Who was the first player to win 100 caps for England?
10. Who was the first Briton to be European Footballer of the Year?

Geography 1 (*Answers on page 163*)
1. Which country consists of over 7,000 islands, the largest of which are Luzon and Mindanao?
2. Which of the Channel Islands is furthest south?
3. Which is the largest of the United Arab Emirates?
4. In which country is Timbuktu?
5. What is the capital of Paraguay?
6. Of which European state is Vaduz the capital?
7. Which European city has its airport in another country?
8. Which of the Great Lakes is entirely within the boundaries of the United States?
9. In which European city is the Atomium?
10. Which is the largest island in the Caribbean?

Geography 2 (*Answers on page 163*)
1. In which continent is Heligoland?
2. Which river runs through Lisbon?
3. In terms of area, which is the world's largest desert?
4. Which republic lies in the Pyrenees between France and Spain?
5. Which European capital city was previously known as Christiania?
6. Which country is divided into two, close to the 38th parallel?
7. Which is the most commonly spoken language in India?
8. In which ocean is Mauritius?
9. In which country is Entebbe, scene of an Israeli com-

mando raid in 1976 to free hi-jacked hostages?

10. In which American State is the United States' highest peak?

Geography 3 (*Answers on page 163*)

1.   What is the State Capital of Texas?
2.   On which Mediterranean island would you find the town of Ajaccio?
3.   In which modern country is the region of Transylvania?
4.   Which Strait separates Australia from Tasmania?
5.   On which of the Great Lakes does Chicago lie?
6.   What is Scotland's longest river?
7.   What name is given to a line on a map connecting places with the same barometric pressure?
8.   In which ocean is the island of St. Helena?
9.   Which island group is separated from the British mainland by the Pentland Firth?
10. Into which sea does the River Volga flow?

Geography 4 (*Answers on page 164*)

1.   What name is given to a line on a map joining places with equal rainfall?
2.   It is an archipelago of 67 islands; it is nearer to Oslo than it is to London, although it is only 6 miles from the Scottish coast. Which group of islands?
3.   In which country are the Plains of Abraham?
4.   Which is the most populated city in the continent of Africa?
5.   Hugh Town is the major town of which group of islands?
6.   In terms of area, which of the following is the largest:– Anglesey, Isle of Man, Isle of Wight?
7.   In which county is England's most easterly point?
8.   In which country would you find the Great Sandy Desert, the Tanami Desert, the Gibson Desert and the Simpson Desert?
9.   Which is the world's longest range of mountains?
10. Which town is the Administrative Headquarters of Lancashire?

Geography 5 (*Answers on page 164*)
1. Cape York is the northernmost point of which Commonwealth country?
2. Which country's capital city lies on the River Jumna?
3. In terms of area, what became the world's largest country after the break-up of the U.S.S.R.?
4. What is the official language of Andorra?
5. By what name are the Sandwich Islands now better known?
6. What is represented by a red triangle on an Ordnance Survey map?
7. Off the coast of which country would you find Queen Charlotte Island?
8. Which is the second most populated country in the world?
9. In which group of islands would you find Lanzarote and Tenerife?
10. Which is the most southerly capital city?

Geography 6 (*Answers on page 164*)
1. Which country in the EC has the highest population?
2. In which English county is most of the Forest of Dean?
3. By what name was the Republic of South Yemen known prior to 1967?
4. By what name is the Boulder Dam on the Colorado River now known?
5. Which European capital city lies on the River Aar?
6. Which was Britain's first National Park?
7. In which country is the Atacama Desert?
8. Which city is dominated by Sugar Loaf Mountain?
9. Which Australian state borders all the other mainland states?
10. In terms of area, which is the world's largest landlocked country?

History 1 (*Answers on page 164*)
1. Who was the Morning Post's correspondent in South Africa during the Boer War?

2.   What did John Bellingham do on 11th May 1812 which resulted in his being hanged?

3.   Who was British Prime Minister at the time of Queen Victoria's death?

4.   Which famous historical character had a horse named Bucephalus?

5.   Against which country did England fight the War of Jenkin's Ear?

6.   Which of Henry VIII's wives was the first to be beheaded?

7.   Captain Edward J. Smith died on 15th April, 1912. What was his claim to fame?

8.   Alongside which river is Pocahontas buried?

9.   Name the ship which was bombed by the R.A.F. off the Cornish coast in 1967.

10.   Which political leader wrote a novel, known in English as 'The Cardinal's Mistress', which was later made into a successful silent movie?

History 2 (*Answers on page 164*)

1.   Which British Prime Minister's wife was also the sister, aunt and mother of three others?

2.   What codename was used by the Germans for their plans to invade the U.S.S.R. in 1941?

3.   Who succeeded Henry VIII?

4.   Who was British Prime Minister at the time of the General Strike?

5.   Which Royal House preceded the House of Stuart?

6.   Who wrote 'The Communist Manifesto' with Karl Marx?

7.   What relation was George the Third to George the Second?

8.   From which country did the U.S.A. buy Louisiana in 1803?

9.   Who succeeded Clement Attlee as leader of the Labour Party in 1955?

10.   Which country was ruled by Bernardo O'Higgins from 1810–1823?

History 3 (*Answers on page 164*)
1. Who was the last English King to die on the battlefield?
2. Where was the capital of the 8th century Kingdom of Wessex?
3. Lambert Simnel and Perkin Warbeck were pretenders to the English throne in whose reign?
4. What relation was Henry VIII to Catherine of Aragon's first husband?
5. Who was U.S. President when Hawaii became an American state?
6. Which British Prime Minister was Rudyard Kipling's brother-in-law?
7. On which Scandinavian country did Britain declare war in December 1941?
8. Who ousted Milton Obote from power in 1971?
9. Which famous military leader's real name was Temujin?
10. How did the suffragette Emily Davidson die in June 1913?

History 4 (*Answers on page 165*)
1. Which public school was founded by Henry VI in 1420 as a preparatory school for Kings College, Cambridge?
2. Which murderer was arrested along with Ethel Le Neve on board the S.S. Montrose in the Gulf of St. Lawrence in 1910, having registered as John Robinson and son?
3. In which town did Martin Luther nail his 95 theses to a church door?
4. Who was the last English monarch to be executed?
5. After the invasion of Poland, which was the next country to be invaded by the Germans in World War II?
6. Which town was known to the Romans as Pons Aelius?
7. Established as a military cemetery in 1864, the Arlington National Cemetery in Virginia stands in the grounds of whose former mansion?
8. From which Oxford College did Margaret Thatcher graduate?
9. Which French king was known as the Sun King?
10. Which famous Greek philosopher was a tutor to Alexander the Great?

History 5 (*Answers on page 165*)
1. Who was the first English Christian martyr?
2. Who was Minister for Health from 1945–1951?
3. Which famous Englishman left England to go to France on board the destroyer 'Fury' on 11 December 1936?
4. Who was appointed Commander-in-Chief of the Royalist forces in 1644, becoming an admiral after the restoration of Charles II?
5. Which engineer designed the Clifton suspension bridge, the ships Great Eastern and Great Western, as well as being chief engineer for the Great Western Railway?
6. Which country was first discovered by the Portuguese Pedro Cabral whilst heading for India in 1500?
7. Who commanded the victorious forces at the Battle of Trasimene in 217 BC and at the Battle of Cannae the following year?
8. Which French king did Henry VIII meet in 1520 at the Field of the Cloth of Gold?
9. Who was the first Roman emperor to be converted to Christianity?
10. Which city was besieged by the Finns to the north and the Germans from the south, from August 1941 until relieved in January 1944?

History 6 (*Answers on page 165*)
1. Who was King Henry VIII's first wife?
2. On which island did Napoleon Bonaparte die?
3. Built by Henry VIII, which London Palace was destroyed by fire in 1698?
4. What was the name of the Roman road that ran from London to Lincoln?
5. Which British King has had the longest reign since 1066?
6. Who crowned Napoleon Bonaparte Emperor in 1804?
7. In which English city was Constantine the Great when he was proclaimed Roman Emperor?
8. Which English architect was responsible for designing both Castle Howard and Blenheim Palace?
9. A former Mayor of Cologne and founder of the Christian

Democrat Party, who was Chancellor of the German Federal Republic from 1949 to 1963?

10. Which island has been ruled over by two King Rogers?

Husbands and Wives (*Answers on page 165*)

1. Who was the first husband of the film star Elizabeth Taylor?
2. Who was the famous wife of Leofric, Earl of Mercia?
3. What was the surname of the couple played by Rock Hudson and Susan St. James in a 1970's TV series?
4. Which actor was the first husband of the actress Jill Ireland?
5. Who was the wife of Menelaus?
6. Mary of Teck was the wife of which British monarch?
7. In the TV series 'Forever Green', who was Pauline Collins' husband, both in the series and in real life?
8. Which poet laureate was married to the poet Sylvia Plath?
9. What is the name of Barney Rubble's wife in the TV cartoon series 'The Flintstones'?
10. Which actress, daughter of Debbie Reynolds, was once married to the singer-songwriter Paul Simon?

Indoor Games (*Answers on page 165*)

1. What number appears on the black ball in a game of pool?
2. In which card game do players 'capture the pack', 'freeze the pack' and 'meld out'?
3. How many coins does a player have in a game of shove halfpenny?
4. How many holes can you pot the ball down on a bar billiards table?
5. How many spots appear in total on a set of dominoes?
6. What score is denoted by the term 'bed and breakfast' in a game of darts?
7. How many 'points' are there on a backgammon board?
8. What is the lowest opening bid in a game of contract bridge?
9. What is the first railway station after 'Go' on a Monopoly board?

10.   In which game does the governing body, FIDE, issue a list
       of Elo ratings for the world's leading players?

International Organisations (*Answers on page 165*)
1.   In which African city, in 1963, was the OAU (Organis-
      ation of African Unity) founded?
2.   In which city are the headquarters of the United Nations?
3.   Which organisation with its headquarters in Geneva, is
      known by its acronym WMO?
4.   Which organisation traces its birth to the Treaty of Rome?
5.   What is the equivalent of the Red Cross in Muslim
      countries?
6.   Which was the only European communist country not to
      have joined the Warsaw Pact when it was formed in 1955?
7.   How many countries are permanent members of the
      United Nations Security Council?
8.   In which country is the European Court of Justice?
9.   Which organisation was founded in 1959 by seven non-
      European Community western European states to
      promote economic expansion?
10.   Which international organisation for humanitarianism,
      founded in Britain in 1961, was awarded the Nobel Peace
      Prize in 1977?

Literary Characters (*Answers on page 165*)
Which authors created the following fictional characters:–
1.   Dracula
2.   The Scarlet Pimpernel
3.   Tommy and Tuppence
4.   Mike Hammer
5.   Gemima Puddleduck
6.   Billy Bunter
7.   Bilbo Baggins
8.   Harry Palmer
9.   Hal 9000
10.   Augustus Snodgrass

Literature 1 (*Answers on page 166*)
1.   In Shakespeare, who were Valentine and Proteus?

2. Which metaphysical poet became Dean of St. Paul's in 1621?

3. Which Russian author wrote the novel 'Dead Souls'?

4. What was the surname of the brothers who wrote 'Diary of a Nobody'?

5. In which Dickens novel would you find the character 'Betsy Trotwood'?

6. Which Shakespearian character was described as 'the noblest Roman of them all'?

7. Which fictional detective had a manservant called Bunter?

8. Which famous English writer was named by his parents after a lake in Staffordshire?

9. Which Poet Laureate wrote detective novels under the pseudonym Nicholas Blake?

10. Which English humorous novelist with the Christian name Pelham, born the year Dostoevsky died, once put on a 50 partnership with Conan Doyle at Lords, spent part of the Second World War staying at the best hotel in Berlin, and died in 1975?

Literature 2 (*Answers on page 166*)

1. Which book was at the centre of the 1960 court case 'Regina v. Penguin Books Ltd.'?

2. For how many years did Rip Van Winkle sleep in the story by Washington Irving?

3. Which famous writer worked as a hospital dispenser during the First World War, thus developing a useful knowledge of poisons?

4. Which writer of the books 'The Moon and Sixpence' and 'Of Human Bondage', trained as a doctor, was made a Commander of the Legion of Honour for his work as a secret agent in World War I, and married the daughter of Dr. Barnardo?

5. James Bond first appeared in which book by Ian Fleming?

6. On which date did Robert Burns celebrate his birthday?

7. Which character in Sheridan's play 'The Rivals' has given her name to the language for someone who misapplies words?

8.   Which one-time San Franciscan detective wrote the book 'The Maltese Falcon'?

9.   What was the name of the dog in Jerome K. Jerome's 'Three Men In A Boat'?

10. How many of Shakespeare's plays have the name 'Henry' in the title?

Literature 3 (Animals) (*Answers on page 166*)

1.   Which fictional character had a horse named Rosinante?

2.   Who wrote the novel 'Black Beauty'?

3.   In P.G. Wodehouse's works, what type of animal was the 'Empress of Blandings'?

4.   What colour was the whale in 'Moby Dick'?

5.   In George Orwell's 'Animal Farm', what type of animal was Boxer?

6.   What was the name of the lion in 'The Lion, the Witch and the Wardrobe' by C.S. Lewis?

7.   What was the pseudonym of the author of 'Bull-dog Drummond'?

8.   In 'Alice's Adventures in Wonderland', what type of birds were used as mallets to play croquet?

9.   In the Sherlock Holmes' story, what type of animal was 'The Speckled Band'?

10. Which is the only Shakespeare play with an animal in its title?

Literature 4 (Authors) (*Answers on page 166*)

Who were the authors of the following works?

1.   The Carpetbaggers

2.   The Waste Land

3.   Slaughterhouse-Five

4.   Brave New World

5.   Catch 22

6.   The Road To Wigan Pier

7.   The Red-Headed League

8.   Robinson Crusoe

9.   Willy Wonka and the Chocolate Factory

10. Gone With The Wind

Literature 5 (Shakespeare) (*Answers on page 166*)

1. Which sport is referred to in 'Antony and Cleopatra'?
2. What is the only Shakespeare play with a British town in the title?
3. Only one Shakespearian play is subtitled. Name either the title *or* the subtitle of that play.
4. Which is the longest of Shakespeare's plays?
5. Which Shakespearian character died on the 15th March?
6. At the end of Macbeth, who becomes king?
7. In Act III of 'The Winter's Tale', the stage directions have Antigonus exiting the stage pursued by what type of animal?
8. Upon which of Shakespeare's plays was the Musical 'West Side Story' based?
9. In which Shakespearian play does a dog 'Crab', appear on stage?
10. In which Shakespearian play would you find a tinker, a tailor, a carpenter, a joiner, a weaver and a bellows-mender?

Middle Names (*Answers on page 166*)

1. Which British athlete, who won Olympic gold medals in 1980 and 1984, has Newbold as his middle name?
2. Which poet and playwright, winner of the 1948 Nobel Prize for Literature, had the middle name Stearns?
3. What was the middle name of the U.S. President, Harry S. Truman?
4. Which English humorous poet, who collaborated in the writing of 14 comic operas, had the middle name Schwenck?
5. The middle names of which member of the royal family are Charles Albert David?
6. Which novelist's middle names were Ronald Reuel?
7. What is the middle name of the ex-Beatle, Paul McCartney?
8. The England Test bowler Bob Willis added an extra middle name during a tour of Australia after attending a concert. What was it?

9. Which writer had the middle names Fingal O'Flahertie Wills?
10. Which British Olympic gold medallist has the forenames Francis Morgan?

Missing Links 1 (*Answers on page 167*)

1. What do the following have in common:–
    Cheviot, Clun Forest, Kerry Hill, Wensleydale?
2. The following are examples of what:–
    Helvetica, Bodoni, Times, Univers?
3. The following are types of what?
    Wilja, Arran Pilot, Pentland Crown, Desiree?
4. Which fictional character has been played on film by the following:–
    Sir Seymour Hicks, Albert Finney, George C. Scott, Reginald Owen, Alistair Sim?
5. The following are varieties of what:–
    Blenheim Orange, Discovery, Jonathan, Grenadier?
6. What do the following have in common:–
    Sir Winston Churchill, Rudyard Kipling, Pearl Buck, William Butler Yeats?
7. Name the song which has been a UK hit for the following artistes:–
    Elvis Presley, The Sex Pistols, Dorothy Squires, Frank Sinatra.
8. The following are varieties of what:–
    Carragheen, Kelp, Bladder-wrack, Laver?
9. Which Olympic event has been won by the following:–
    Spiridon Louis, Abebe Bikila, Frank Shorter, Carlos Lopez?
10. What have the following got in common:–
    Dong, Colon, Sucre, Lempira?

Missing Links 2 (*Answers on page 167*)

1. With what would you associate the following:–
    Cups, Swords, Wands, Pentacles?
2. Which British Cabinet post has been held by the following:–

Winston Churchill, Roy Jenkins, Nigel Lawson, Anthony Barber?
3. The following are varieties of what:–
   Hampshire, Yorkshire, Wessex Saddleback, Tamworth?
4. What have the following dates got in common:–
   1st March, 17th March, 23rd April, 30th November?
5. What do the following have in common:–
   French, Sicilian, Slav, Caro-Kahn?
6. What, in particular, do the following have in common:–
   Monkey, Snake, Rat, Dragon?
7. What have the following in common:–
   Omaha, Sword, Utah, Juno?
8. The following are varieties of what:–
   Boudin Blanc, Weisswurst, Pepperoni, Chorizo?
9. What do the following have in common:–
   Fan, Mitre, Candle, Lily?
10. The following are varieties of which animal:–
   Shoveler, Pochard, Khaki Campbell, Canvasback?

Missing Links 3 (*Answers on page 167*)
1. In which Shakespeare play would you find the following characters:–
   Antonio, Miranda, Trinculo, Ariel?
2. The following are types of what:–
   Comma, Swallowtail, Brimstone, Cardinal?
3. The following are varieties of what:–
   Pekoe, Lady Londonderry, Green Gunpowder, Oolong?
4. The following are varieties of what:–
   Blue Brindles, Common Reds, Flettons, London Stock?
5. Which item comes in the following sizes:–
   Double-Crown, Octavo, A2, B4?
6. What do the following have in common:–
   Tishri, Kislev, Tevet, Av?
7. What do the following have in common:–
   Dunlop, Samsoe, Cornish Yarg, Cotherstone?
8. With which literary group would you associate the following:–
   Nathaniel Winkle, Tracy Tupman, Augustus Snodgrass?

9.   Which pop artiste would you associate with the following groups:–
     Bubblerock, Sakkarin, 100 Ton and a Feather, The Weathermen?
10. The following are examples of what:–
     Bishop Rock, Eddystone, Longstone, Flamborough?

Missing Links 4 (*Answers on page 167*)
1.   With which activity would you associate the following:–
     Bhakti, Karma, Hatha, Raja?
2.   What do the following have in common:–
     Central, Mountain, Pacific, Eastern?
3.   With which composer would you associate the following symphonies:–
     Farewell, London, Clock, Surprise?
4.   What do the following have in common?
     Konrad Adenauer, Uncle Walter, Penelope Keith, Queen Elizabeth?
5.   The following are types of what:–
     Anellini, Ditalini, Fideli, Lumachine?
6.   The following are types of what:–
     Round Head, Oval Head, Diamond Head?
7.   Which famous British race has been won by the following horses:–
     Nijinsky, Bustino, Commanche Run, Touching Wood?
8.   The following are types of what:–
     Charolais, Galloway, Limousin, Welsh Black?
9.   What do the following places have in common:–
     Toddington, Fleet, Membury, Michael Wood?
10. Name the Irving Berlin song which has been a UK Top Fifty hit for the following artistes:–
     Mantovani, Freddie Starr, Bing Crosby, Keith Harris and Orville?

Music 1 (*Answers on page 167*)
1.   Which artiste released a successful LP in 1986 named after Elvis Presley's mansion in Memphis?

2. Who composed 'Black, Brown and Beige' in 1943, and 'Such Sweet Thunder' in 1957?

3. What was Buddy Holly's only number one British hit single?

4. He lived from 1819 to 1895 and in 1857 he founded a series of concerts in Manchester that were named after him. Who was he?

5. Which pop group was named after a character played by Milo O'Shea in the film 'Barbarella'?

6. What nationality was the composer Sibelius?

7. Which patriotic piece of music was composed by Thomas Arne as part of his masque 'Alfred'?

8. Who founded both the London Philharmonic and the Royal Philharmonic Orchestras?

9. What was the title of the 1974 Abba hit single, also the winner of the Eurovision Song Contest?

10. Name the song written by Lennon and McCartney which was a hit for Marianne Faithfull, Ray Charles and Matt Monro before becoming a big hit for the Beatles in 1976.

Music 2 (*Answers on page 167*)

1. Nicknamed the 'March King', who composed 'The Stars and Stripes Forever'?

2. Which record was Cliff Richard's first UK number one hit single?

3. Which soap opera star featured with Mike Sarne on a 1962 UK number one hit?

4. With which famous actor did David Bowie have a big UK hit in 1982 with 'Peace on Earth – Little Drummer Boy'?

5. How many strings are there on an orchestral harp?

6. Which singer and songwriter was born on May 24th 1941, in Duluth, Minnesota?

7. What was the title of The Rolling Stones' first UK number one hit single?

8. Who wrote the musicals 'Annie Get Your Gun' and 'Call Me Madam'?

9. Which of Beethoven's symphonies is called the Pastoral?

10. Name the track from the musical 'Carousel' that was a number one hit in both 1963 and 1985, as well as entering the charts in 1968 when recorded by Elvis Presley.

Music 3 (*Answers on page 168*)
1.   Whose first UK No. 1 hit was 'Into the Groove' in 1985?
2.   By what popular name is Schubert's Eighth Symphony better known?
3.   With which instrument would you associate Charlie Mingus?
4.   Which pop group released two top-selling albums named after Marx Brothers films?
5.   Which group did Sid Vicious leave to join the Sex Pistols?
6.   What is the smallest instrument in the woodwind section of a symphony orchestra?
7.   Who composed 'The Trumpet Voluntary'?
8.   Who composed the symphonies 'Symphonie Fantastique', 'Harold in Italy' and 'Romeo and Juliet'?
9.   Who composed the music to 'West Side Story'?
10. Other than 'She Loves You', in which other Beatles number one hit can you hear the words 'She loves you, yeah, yeah, yeah'?

Music 4 (*Answers on page 168*)
1.   Which record was Elvis Presley's first UK number one?
2.   Who wrote the music to Kismet?
3.   Who was the first artiste to actually receive a gold record for selling a million copies of one title?
4.   Which term is used to describe a piece of music to be performed slowly and leisurely?
5.   Which artiste played harmonica on the 1964 single 'My Boy Lollipop', sang lead vocals on Python Lee Jackson's 1972 single 'In a Broken Dream', as well as having a hit in 1973 with Jeff Beck entitled 'I've Been Drinking'?
6.   Which duo originally released records under the name 'Tom and Jerry'?
7.   What was the title of the first record ever played on Radio One?

8. Which composer adapted 'War and Peace' as an opera?
9. In Holst's Planet Suite, which planet is the bringer of peace?
10. Which was the first Beatles single to make number one in the UK charts?

Music 5 (*Answers on page 168*)
1. Who partnered Elton John on the 1976 UK number one hit entitled 'Don't Go Breaking My Heart'?
2. In music, what is the correct term applied to the playing of a violin by plucking the strings by the fingers rather than using a bow?
3. With which instrument would you especially associate Miles Davis and Dizzy Gillespie?
4. Two members of which pop group wrote the music for the musical 'Chess'?
5. What was the real first name of the jazz musician 'Bix' Beiderbecke?
6. Who wrote the opera 'The Barber of Seville'?
7. Which successful singer has also had hits with Phil Everley, Sarah Brightman, Olivia Newton-John and Elton John?
8. Which work by Gilbert and Sullivan is subtitled 'The Peer and the Peri'?
9. Who composed the opera 'Oedipus Rex'?
10. In Britain, how many copies of a single need to be sold before a gold disc is awarded?

Music 6 (*Answers on page 168*)
1. How many actual strings are there in a standard string quartet?
2. Which composer wrote the operas 'The Pearl Fishers' and 'The Fair Maid of Perth'?
3. Which former bus driver had hits in the sixties with 'Portrait of My Love' as well as a cover version of 'Yesterday'?
4. The subject of a film directed by Ken Russell, which composer was the father-in-law of Richard Wagner?

5. Which artiste performed most of the music for the 1989 film 'Batman'?

6. In the song 'The Twelve Days of Christmas', how many drummers were drumming?

7. In which opera does the heroine work in a cigarette factory?

8. In which country was Cliff Richard born?

9. Which record label was established by Berry Gordy in 1959?

10. Which group, who had a UK number one hit in the 1980's, were named after a character in TV's 'Star Trek'?

Music 7 (*Answers on page 168*)

1. Which artiste had a UK number one hit in 1978 with her first single, named after a novel by Emily Brontë?

2. Which Welsh composer wrote 'Keep the Home Fires Burning'?

3. Who first won the Eurovision Song Contest for Britain?

4. Which American composer wrote 'Appalachian Story' and 'Fanfare For The Common Man', and won an Oscar for his musical score to the 1949 film 'The Heiress'?

5. Which American singer's real name is Noah Kamimsky?

6. What was the title of the track on the reverse side of Boney M's 'Brown Girl In The Ring'?

7. Which novel by Graham Greene has been turned into an opera by Malcolm Williamson?

8. The music of which punk group supplied Keith Floyd with the opening music to his TV series 'Floyd on Food'?

9. Which former night club pianist and accompanist to Marlene Dietrich, composed the songs 'What's New Pussycat', 'Raindrops Keep Fallin' On My Head' and 'I'll Never Fall In Love Again'?

10. Name any three of the five hit singles released by the Beatles in the UK with women's names in the title.

Music and Films (*Answers on page 168*)

1. Which instrument was played by Anton Karas for the theme music of the film 'The Third Man'?

2. The theme music to the films 'E.T.' and 'The Deer Hunter' were UK hits for which two artistes who shared the same name?

3. Who was the first artiste to have sung the title music to *two* James Bond films?

4. In which film did Bill Haley's 'Rock Around the Clock' first feature?

5. Who sang the song 'Pinball Wizard' in the 1975 film 'Tommy', and had a UK Top Ten hit with it the following year?

6. Who sang the song 'I Talk To The Trees' in the 1969 film 'Paint Your Wagon'?

7. What is the *full* title of the film whose title music – 'Eye of the Tiger' by Survivor – was a UK number one hit in 1982?

8. Which film marked Elvis Presley's screen debut?

9. Which actor played the part of Paul McCartney's grandfather in the film 'A Hard Day's Night'?

10. The life of which famous composer was portrayed in Ken Russell's 1971 film 'The Music Lovers'?

Mythology 1 (*Answers on page 168*)

1. In Roman mythology, who was the father of Romulus and Remus?

2. In Norse mythology, whose chariot was drawn across the sky by two goats, called Toothgrinder and Toothgnasher?

3. By what collective name are Medusa, Stheno and Euryale known?

4. Who was given the gift of prophecy by Apollo, although no-one ever believed them?

5. What was the name of the three-headed dog that guarded the gates to Hades?

6. The Egyptian god Anubis had the head of which animal?

7. In Greek mythology, from which race of people did Polyphemus come?

8. Who ferried the dead across the River Styx into Hades?

9. In Roman mythology Mercury was messenger of the gods. Who was messenger of the gods in Greek mythology?

10. According to legend, who founded Carthage?

Mythology 2 (*Answers on page 169*)
1.   Which bird is associated with the Greek Goddess Athena?
2.   Who was the illegitimate son of Ilgraine and Uther Pendragon?
3.   Who was the twin brother of the goddess Artemis?
4.   With which country would you associate the legendary figures Bran, Bres and Febal?
5.   In Homer's Odyssey, into which type of creature did Circe turn Odysseus' men?
6.   Which legendary Greek craftsman built the Labyrinth?
7.   What was the name of the monster killed by Beowulf?
8.   Which Roman god had two faces?
9.   Of which country was Midas the king?
10. Who was the Greek god of the sea?

Mythology 3 (*Answers on page 169*)
1.   In Greek mythology, what was the food of the gods?
2.   Which legendary Greek hero killed the Gorgon, Medusa?
3.   Who was King of Troy during the famous siege?
4.   Assisted by Ariadne, who killed the minotaur?
5.   What was the name of the ancient Egyptian sun god?
6.   Which Spaniard did the Aztecs think was their god Quetzacoatl?
7.   In Greek mythology, what was the name of Bellerophon's horse?
8.   Who is said to have given fire to mankind after stealing it from the gods?
9.   What type of wild animal is said to have killed the beautiful youth Adonis?
10. Which is the only Roman god to have had a planet and a day of the week named after him?

Natural History (*Answers on page 169*)
1.   What sort of animals are bobolinks?
2.   What name is given to the art of trimming shrubs and hedges into ornamental shapes?
3.   By what name do we know the bird Pica Pica?

4. From which country does the Monkey Puzzle tree originate?
5. By what name is the plant heartsease better known?
6. What sort of animal is a coelocanth?
7. The young of which animal are referred to as 'joeys' by Australians?
8. What name is given to a person who studies or collects shells?
9. By what name is the plant impatiens better known?
10. What unique feature do the young of the South American bird, the hoatzin, have on their wings?

Newspapers (*Answers on page 169*)
1. On what colour paper is the Financial Times traditionally printed?
2. Which American newspaper first exposed the Watergate Affair?
3. Which British newspaper was originally called the 'Daily Universal Register'?
4. What was the previous title of the 'Morning Star'?
5. In which country is the newspaper 'La Stampa' published?
6. Which is the oldest British national Sunday newspaper?
7. What was the name of the newspaper featured in the TV series 'Lou Grant', starring Ed Asner?
8. Which British national newspaper launched a Sunday version in 1961?
9. In which British newspaper does the cartoon strip 'Andy Capp' appear?
10. The colour supplement of which national Sunday newspaper is called 'You'?

Numbers (*Answers on page 169*)
1. In the United States of America, if you were given a quarter, a cent, two dimes, and a nickel, how many cents in total would you have been given?
2. How many players are there in an Australian Rules football team?
3. How many 'Red Balloons' did Nena have in the pop charts

in 1984?

4. In the title of the 1963 film about the Boxer Rebellion starring Charlton Heston, Ava Gardner and David Niven, how many days were spent at Peking?

5. How many cards comprise a pack of Tarot cards?

6. What is the number of the unit that appears in the TV series of MASH?

7. According to the Bible, how many Horsemen of the Apocalypse are there?

8. How many symphonies did Beethoven compose?

9. How many fences are jumped in the Grand National?

10. What do the Roman numerals MCLXV represent?

Parliament (*Answers on page 169*)

1. Which parliamentarian sits on the Woolsack?

2. Who was the original printer of 'Parliamentary Debates', a verbatim record of parliamentary speeches?

3. Who was the last British monarch to refuse to give the Royal Assent to a bill passed by parliament?

4. What colour are the seats in the House of Lords?

5. How many people constitute a quorum in the House of Commons?

6. The holder of which Cabinet post receives the highest salary?

7. Who is acknowledged as Britain's first Prime Minister, in office from 1721–42?

8. Who was disqualified from being MP for Bristol South-East in 1960 after inheriting the title Viscount Stansgate upon his father's death?

9. Who was British Prime Minister when MPs were first paid a salary?

10. Who is the only Lord Chancellor to have been canonised?

Quotations (*Answers on page 169*)

Who said the following:–

1. 'The reports of my death are greatly exaggerated.'

2. 'Genius is one percent inspiration and ninety-nine percent perspiration.'

3. 'Please accept my resignation. I don't want to belong to any club that will accept me as a member.'
4. 'It's not the men you see me with. It's the men you don't see me with.'
5. 'Ich bin ein berliner.'
6. 'Marriage has many pains, but celibacy has no pleasures.'
7. 'I have nothing to offer but blood, toil, tears and sweat.'
8. 'When I am dead and opened, you shall find "Calais" lying in my heart.'
9. 'Veni, vidi, vici.'
10. 'There will be no whitewash at the White House.'

Radio and Television 1 (*Answers on page 170*)

1. In the radio comedy series starring Tommy Handley, what did the initials 'ITMA' stand for?
2. Which long-running British TV soap opera had its last showing in April 1988?
3. In the TV series 'Yes, Minister', which department was headed by Jim Hacker before he became Prime Minister?
4. Which puppet appeared on BBC television from 1952 to 1967, and then reappeared on ITV with its deviser's son?
5. Name the *actor* who played the same role in both the television series, and the 1973 film version, of M.A.S.H.
6. What was the title of the 70's TV series which starred Julie Covington, Rula Lenska, Charlotte Cornwell and Sue Jones-Davies as 'The Little Ladies'?
7. How many records are selected by each castaway on 'Desert Island Discs'?
8. What was the full name of the character played by Ronnie Barker in the series 'Porridge'?
9. Which former TV newsreader wrote the thrillers 'Harry's Game' and 'The Glory Boys', later adapted for television?
10. Which actor played the title role in the TV series 'The Irish R.M.'?

Radio and Television 2 (*Answers on page 170*)

1. In which town did the cartoon family 'The Flintstones' live?

2. How many books did each castaway have with them in the original version of 'Desert Island Discs'?

3. Which pair were played on TV by Adam West and Burt Ward?

4. Which TV comedian was famous for wearing a fez?

5. In the 1980's, who narrated TV's 'Thomas the Tank Engine'?

6. Which IBA local radio station is based around the Manchester area?

7. What was Patrick McGoohan's number in the 1960's TV series 'The Prisoner'?

8. In which American city is Dynasty set?

9. At the start and finish of which TV programme would you hear the music entitled 'Approaching Menace'?

10. On which sixties TV music programme did Janice Nichols make her mark with the line 'I'll buy it, and give it five!'?

Radio and Television 3 (*Answers on page 170*)

1. Of which company was Richard De Vere the Chairman in 'To The Manor Born'?

2. Who took over from Bob Monkhouse on the TV programme 'Family Fortunes'?

3. Who was the first Disc Jockey to be heard on Radio One?

4. In which TV series did Patrick McGoohan star as John Drake?

5. What is the surname of the character played by Kevin Whately in the TV programme 'Inspector Morse'?

6. Whom did Sarah Kennedy replace as host of 'Busman's Holiday'?

7. Which TV character is a postal worker with a cat called Jess?

8. Who played the bounty hunter Josh Randall in the TV series 'Wanted Dead or Alive'?

9. In the original series of Star Trek, what was Captain Kirk's middle name?

10. In which T.V. series did Stefanie Powers star as April Dancer?

Rivers (*Answers on page 170*)
Name the main river which runs through the following towns:–
1. Cambridge
2. Nottingham
3. Derby
4. Cardiff
5. Preston
6. Lincoln
7. Kings Lynn
8. Yeovil
9. Chester
10. Canterbury

Science 1 (*Answers on page 170*)
1. H_2SO_4 is the chemical formula of which acid?
2. What is made in a Bessemer Converter?
3. Name *both* the constituents of brass.
4. Which planet was discovered by William Herschell in 1781?
5. Which silvery-white metal has the atomic number 19, and the symbol 'K'?
6. How is −40 (minus forty degrees) Centigrade expressed on the Fahrenheit scale?
7. What is the hardest naturally occurring substance known to man?
8. Other than gold and silver, which other metal is hall-marked in Britain?
9. What, in the human body, is the patella?
10. What is the cube root of 729?

Science 2 (*Answers on page 170*)
1. Which scientist's Three Laws of Motion were first published in 1687 in the book 'Principia'?
2. What is studied by a mycologist?
3. What is the more common name for the disease 'varicella'?
4. In radio, FM stands for frequency modulation, but what does AM stand for?

5.   What would be studied by an icthyologist?
6.   What is the chemical symbol for tin?
7.   Pyrotechnics is the art or craft of making what?
8.   On the Reaumur scale, what is the boiling point of water?
9.   Which is the smallest planet in the solar system?
10. Which scientist discovered polonium in 1898?

Science 3 (*Answers on page 171*)
1.   In which South African city did the first human heart transplant operation take place in 1967?
2.   What is the more usual name for oil of vitriol?
3.   Which part of the body is affected by gingivitis?
4.   Which vitamin is otherwise called ascorbic acid?
5.   What is the more common name for magnesium sulphate?
6.   Which gas is the most abundant constituent of air?
7.   In computing terminology, what does the acronym ROM stand for?
8.   How many faces does a tetrahedron have?
9.   The orbit of which planet in the solar system lies between Mars and Venus?
10. What is the name of the southern hemisphere's equivalent of the Aurora Borealis?

Science 4 (*Answers on page 171*)
1.   What nationality was the astronomer Nicolaus Copernicus?
2.   What is the positive heavy particle of the nucleus of an atom called?
3.   Which element has the chemical symbol Pt?
4.   On which planet would you find the Great Red Spot?
5.   What name is given to a triangle where two of its three sides are the same length?
6.   What medical condition is otherwise known as epistaxis?
7.   Which gas was used in the German airship the Hindenburg?
8.   Whose 'law' states that if the temperature of a fixed mass of gas is constant, then the pressure and volume of the gas are inversely proportional?

9. Which unit is equal to the amount of heat necessary to raise the temperature of 1 gram of water 1 degree Centigrade?

10. Which German scientist was the first ever winner of the Nobel Prize for Physics for his discovery of X Rays?

Sport 1 *(Answers on page 171)*

1. Which popular female show-jumper died during a competition in 1983?
2. Which sport requires stones to be thrown at houses?
3. What colour jacket does the greyhound from trap one wear?
4. Which non-Alpine sport takes place on the piste?
5. What is the combined distance of the two Classic horseraces, the Derby and the Oaks?
6. What sporting 'first' was achieved by Susan Brown in 1981?
7. What is the nickname of the football league club that plays at the Dell?
8. How many players in a polo team?
9. Which cricket team plays at Grace Road?
10. In golf, what would be your score if you scored an albatross on a par five hole?

Sport 2 *(Answers on page 171)*

1. In a game of snooker, how many consecutive 'pots' must be made to score a maximum 147 break?
2. If one team were playing with blue and black balls, whilst their opponents were playing with yellow and red balls, which sport would they be playing?
3. For which county did the famous cricketer, Doctor W.G. Grace, play?
4. In which weight division did Muhammad Ali (or Cassius Clay, as he was then called) win an Olympic Gold Medal?
5. How many innings are there in a baseball match?
6. Who was the first women's gold medallist in the Olympic marathon?
7. With which sport would you associate Beryl Burton and Reg Harris?

8. Who were the first non-English team to win the F.A. Cup?
9. The Indianapolis 500 consists of how many laps?
10. Name *all* three sports in which the winners *must* go backwards.

Sport 3 (*Answers on page 171*)

1. In 1886, which team equalled the record set by Wanderers of having won three successive F.A. Cup finals?
2. Which modern sport developed from the game 'gossima'?
3. Which of the following sports can have the widest pitch:– Association Football, Rugby League, Rugby Union, Lacrosse?
4. In 1930, which cricketer became the first player to score more than 300 runs in a single innings in a test match against England?
5. At which winter resort would you find the Cresta Run?
6. Which sport was devised by Dr. James Naismith in Massachusetts in 1891, becoming an Olympic sport for men in 1936 and for women in 1976?
7. Which team sport can only be played right-handed?
8. Who was the first British woman to win the Wimbledon singles tennis championship after World War II?
9. What is the middle discipline in a triathlon?
10. With all three darts scoring, what is the lowest number (above three) that cannot be scored?

Sport 4 (*Answers on page 171*)

1. Who was the first female jockey to ride in the Grand National?
2. In 1967, which golfer made the first televised hole-in-one?
3. How many players in a baseball team?
4. On his twenty-eighth attempt to win that race, which jockey rode Pinza to win the 1953 English Derby?
5. Which football team, a member of the Scottish league, has their home ground in England?
6. In which year were the Olympic Games first held in London?

7.   In which event did the Britons Nash and Dixon win a gold medal at the 1964 Winter Olympics?
8.   Who became the World Heavyweight Boxing Champion after the retirement of Rocky Marciano?
9.   In the darts game '501', what is the least number of darts needed for a player to 'check out'?
10. Name three of the four English football league clubs with an 'X' in their name.

Sport 5 (*Answers on page 172*)
1.   Which Briton never won the Formula One World Drivers Championship, although he came second in four successive years from 1955 to 1958?
2.   Which was the first English football league club to install an artificial pitch?
3.   In snooker, what is the points value of the green ball?
4.   Which British racecourse stages *only one* of the English horse-race Classics?
5.   Which was the first city in the southern hemisphere to host the Olympic Games?
6.   Which sport is governed by the I.S.U.?
7.   Which major British sporting trophy is made from melted down coins?
8.   How many people compete in the annual University Boat Race?
9.   In showjumping, how many faults are incurred for the first refusal?
10. Name an Olympic sport which imposes a *maximum* age limit upon competitors.

Sport 6 (*Answers on page 172*)
1.   In football, a game starts with a kick-off. What is the equivalent in ice hockey?
2.   Hampden Park is the home ground of which Scottish league football club?
3.   How many fences are jumped only once by the winner of the Grand National at Aintree?
4.   Which game was originally called 'Poona'?

5. Who was the first professional boxer to win world titles at four different weight divisions?
6. Which English football league club is the furthest north?
7. In which sport would a toxophilist compete?
8. In rugby league, what is the total playing time of each game?
9. At which British racecourse is the Lincolnshire Handicap run?
10. How many dead heats were there in the first hundred University Boat Races?

Sport 7 (*Answers on page 172*)
1. In which sport might you get classes called 'Tornado', 'Star' and 'Flying Dutchman'?
2. Chris Brasher, who had helped pace-make Roger Bannister's first sub-four minute mile and who later became Race Director for the London Marathon, won a gold medal at the 1956 Olympics in which event?
3. Which world champion at table tennis went on to win the Wimbledon Singles Lawn Tennis title five years later?
4. How many bridges does the course of the University Boat Race pass under?
5. Which 18-a-side ball game is played on an oval pitch?
6. Which sport, at international level, is played by teams of ten in men's events but teams of twelve in women's events?
7. In which sport are the Thomas Cup and the Uber Cup competed for?
8. What is the last discipline in a heptathlon?
9. Other than Newcastle United, which other league football club's home ground is called St. James Park?
10. Which British rider rode Laurieston to win the 1972 Olympic gold medal for the Individual Three-Day Event?

Sport 8 (*Answers on page 172*)
1. Who were the last non-league winners of the F.A. Cup?
2. Who was the trainer of the triple Grand National winner, Red Rum?
3. From which U.S. city do the American football team, the 49ers, come?

4. Which county has won cricket's county championship the most times?
5. Who partnered John McEnroe to four Wimbledon Doubles titles between 1979 and 1984?
6. Which sporting trophy was first competed for by 15 teams, including Hitchin, Great Marlow, Hampstead Heathens and Harrow Chequers?
7. Which was the first football club to have won the F.A. Cup on seven occasions?
8. Whom did England defeat in the semi-final of the 1966 football World Cup?
9. For which team did James Hunt race in 1976, the year he became Formula One World Champion?
10. Who was the first man to have been both 500cc World Motor Cycling Champion *and* Formula One Motor Racing World Champion?

Sport 9 (*Answers on page 172*)
1. Other than Geoff Hurst, who else scored for England in the 1966 World Cup final?
2. Which 6–a–side Olympic sport was invented in 1895 by William Morgan, and was originally called 'Mintonette'?
3. Which English football team were the first this century to achieve the league and cup double?
4. Which football team play at 'Filbert Street'?
5. Who was the first boxer to defeat Cassius Clay/ Muhammad Ali?
6. By what name are the touring New Zealand rugby league team called?
7. In yards, what is the maximum permitted length of a soccer pitch?
8. Which sport traces its development back to an invention by George Nissen in 1936?
9. For which event did the City Police, representing Great Britain, win a gold medal at the 1908 Olympic Games?
10. If you had a polo team and a basketball team, how many more players would you need to make a full rugby union team?

Sport and Games (*Answers on page 172*)

1. In which sport or game are the Bermuda Bowl (for men) and the Venice Trophy (for women) recognised as the world team championships?

2. In which sport or game would you find classes called K1, K2, C1 and C2?

3. In which sport or game are the Swaythling and Corbillon Cups competed for?

4. In which sport or game was Emanuel Lasker world champion from 1894 to 1921?

5. In which sport or game was a score of 42,746 recorded by William Cook in 1907?

6. In which sport or game have Milan, Dynamo Tbilisi, Cibona Zagreb and Real Madrid all been European champions?

7. In which sport or game were Djibouti the winners of the men's world team championship in 1985?

8. In which sport or game are only two of the seven players in each team allowed to score?

9. In which sport or game did Alice Blanche Legh win her 23rd British ladies title at the age of 67?

10. In which sport or game is there a net 5 foot high, and a court up to 44' by 20'?

Television Title Roles (*Answers on page 172*)

Name the actor who played the original title role in each of the following TV series:–

1. Lovejoy
2. Worzel Gummidge
3. The Fall Guy
4. Robin's Nest
5. Yes, Minister
6. Ironside
7. Shoestring
8. The Rockford Files
9. Columbo
10. Adam Adamant

Travel (*Answers on page 173*)
1.   On which Mediterranean island is the town of Iraklion?
2.   Which is the largest of the Balearic Islands?
3.   What is the name of the Dutch national airline?
4.   Name the only country which has parts on the mainland of both Europe and Africa?
5.   Which Irish city is served by Shannon airport?
6.   On which sea is the resort of Rimini?
7.   In which British seaside resort would you find a famous area called 'the Lancs'?
8.   In which European country is the winter resort of Zermatt?
9.   IS are the international car identification letters for cars from which country?
10.   Which European capital city has a main line railway station named after a battle of 1805?

Wars (*Answers on page 173*)
Which wars were fought between the following dates:–
1.   1914 – 1918
2.   1899 – 1902
3.   1870 – 1871
4.   1950 – 1953
5.   1861 – 1865
6.   1904 – 1905
7.   1854 – 1856
8.   1775 – 1781
9.   1936 – 1939
10.   1839 – 1842

Who? (*Answers on page 173*)
1.   Which engineer built the Caledonian Canal, the Menai Suspension Bridge and The Gotha Canal in Sweden?
2.   Born on the borders of Albania and Yugoslavia in 1910, who won the Nobel Peace Prize in 1979?
3.   Which Norwegian dramatist wrote the play Peer Gynt?
4.   Who succeeded Brezhnev as president of the USSR in 1982?

5.   An ambulance driver in the First World War and a war correspondent in the Second World War, which Nobel Literature prize winner shot himself in 1961?
6.   Which English theologian founded Methodism?
7.   What was Kim Philby's real first name?
8.   By what name is Martha Jane Canary remembered?
9.   Which New Zealand physicist was the first to split the atom in the 1920's?
10. Who wrote the words to 'Auld Lang Syne'?

General Knowledge Quick Questions (*Answers on page 173*)
1.   What is the musical note that equals half a crotchet?
2.   Who wrote 'The Mill on the Floss'?
3.   Which country left the Commonwealth in 1972?
4.   Who created Winnie the Pooh?
5.   What is the southern-most point on the British mainland?
6.   Which actor wrote 'The Moon's a Balloon'?
7.   How many feet are there in one fathom?
8.   In which English county are the Isles of Sheppey and Thanet?
9.   Which planet was not discovered until 1930?
10. Which craft is Honiton noted for?
11. How many times was Franklin D. Roosevelt elected U.S. President?
12. In which pantomime does Widow Twankey appear?
13. What is the total cost of purchasing all four railway stations in an English game of 'Monopoly'?
14. In which famous science-fiction film did Leonard Rossiter have a small part as a Russian scientist?
15. Which philosopher coined the phrase 'I think, therefore I am'?
16. Which comedian's real name was Charles Springall?
17. Outside of which South American city was the Graf Spee scuttled in 1939?
18. In a game of Scrabble, how many bonus points are awarded to a player who uses all their seven letters in one go?
19. The Victoria Cross has which colour ribbon?

20. The name of which European capital city is derived from the names of two towns on either bank of its main river?

21. What is the cube root of 343?

22. In which modern country was Christopher Columbus born?

23. Who wrote the song 'I'm Dreaming of a White Christmas'?

24. Which order of monks are known as the Greyfriars?

25. Which English cathedral has the tallest spire?

26. What name is given to the home of a badger?

27. Which American author created the character 'Rip Van Winkle'?

28. What is the most common blood group in the world?

29. Which actress won an Oscar for her leading role in the 1969 film 'The Prime of Miss Jean Brodie'?

30. In the Bible, who was Isaac's father?

31. How wide is a soccer goal?

32. In which country is the city of Trieste?

33. What name is given to a female swan?

34. Who was the founder of the Church of Scientology?

35. Which English city did the Romans call Deva?

36. Which country held the 1998 Winter Olympics?

37. If you were pyrophobic, of what would you be afraid?

38. What is the capital of Syria?

39. Who would wear The Fisherman's Ring?

40. From which London terminus would you catch a direct non-stop train to Gatwick Airport?

41. How many pairs of ribs would a normal human have?

42. Who wrote the classic novel 'Les Misérables'?

43. What was the name of Sherlock Holmes' housekeeper?

44. Which actress played the part of Sybil Fawlty in television's 'Fawlty Towers'?

45. What was the title of Beethoven's only opera?

46. Which river flows through the city of Dublin?

47. Who appeared with David McCallum in the title role of the TV series 'Sapphire and Steel'?

48. Which Irishman won the Tour de France in 1987?

49. In which country is Cromagnon, famous for the discovery of four palaeolithic skeletons in 1868?

50. Which town is the administrative centre for the Open University?
51. In the nursery rhyme, name *both* items being eaten by Little Miss Muffet.
52. Which river flows through Rome?
53. In which British city is the Crucible Theatre, famous for hosting snooker tournaments?
54. In which European capital city is the Christiansborg Palace?
55. In the USA, how many cents make a dime?
56. In the film 'Bambi', what type of animal was Thumper?
57. A Ruby Wedding Anniversary celebrates how many years?
58. Who was the Minister of Transport responsible for the introduction of the breathalyser in 1967?
59. In which country did the composer Sergei Rachmaninov die in 1943?
60. How many pairs of chromosomes does a human have?
61. What was the venue of the first F.A. Cup Final in 1872?
62. In which Italian city would you find the Bridge of Sighs?
63. Which English novelist wrote 'Brideshead Revisited'?
64. Which English football league club play at Maine Road?
65. Which British monarch did Queen Victoria succeed?
66. In which year were the first modern Olympic games held?
67. What is the name of Chicago's international airport?
68. Cars from which country have the letters 'CH' on them?
69. Which U.S. state is nicknamed the 'Cotton State'?
70. What colour is the starboard light on a ship?
71. What is the name of the ruling house of Monaco?
72. What is the official residence of the Lord Mayor of London?
73. In World War Two, the Home Guard were originally known as the L.D.V. What did this stand for?
74. How many operas make up Wagner's 'Ring Cycle'?
75. In bookmaker's slang, how much does a 'monkey' and a 'pony' add up to?
76. What was made, and sold, by a fletcher?
77. Noddy Holder was the lead singer of which 1970's pop group?

78. Which building stands on 5th Avenue and 34th Street in New York?
79. What name is given to a male rabbit?
80. Who is the patron saint of children?
81. Who wrote 'The Wind in the Willows'?
82. Who starred with Jon Voight in the film 'Midnight Cowboy'?
83. Which country drew 0–0 with England in the opening match of the 1966 World Cup Finals?
84. What is the shortest race distance under Jockey Club rules?
85. Whom did Fidel Castro replace as Cuban leader in 1959?
86. In the 1920's who was responsible for the structure of two airships, the R80 and R100, and in the 1930's for the design of two long-range bombers, the Wellesley and the Wellington?
87. In 1939, Britain's largest Opera House was opened. In which town was it?
88. Which title did the motor car manufacturer William Morris take when he was created a Viscount?
89. Which of the Beatles was left-handed?
90. Which English city holds a Goose Fair each year in October?
91. For which rugby union club did both Barry John and Phil Bennett play?
92. For which crime was Konrad Kujau jailed in 1984?
93. What is the name of Dennis the Menace's dog?
94. What is the main food of the giant panda?
95. Which Scottish clan were the victims of the Massacre at Glencoe?
96. In the Bible, who was the brother of Aaron?
97. Which fictional character tilted at windmills?
98. To whom did Beethoven dedicate his Third Symphony?
99. What is 25% of two gross?
100. What is the common English name of the plant myosotis?
101. On board ship, how long is a Dog Watch?
102. What is agoraphobia the fear of?
103. Which type of book would be written by a lexicographer?

104. How many years marriage is celebrated in a Pearl Wedding?
105. Which sign of the Zodiac is represented by the Ram?
106. Which show-jumper became World Champion on Beethoven and European Champion on both Sunsalve and Mister Softee?
107. In which galaxy is the Earth?
108. Where in the human body would you find the malleus?
109. Horses are often measured in 'hands'. How many inches are there in a hand?
110. Name the only U.S. state beginning with the letter 'D'.
111. What is the fruit of a beech tree known as?
112. What is the official title of the person popularly referred to as the Ombudsman?
113. How many months of the year have 30 or more days?
114. What is the fourth book of the Old Testament?
115. In which ocean is Christmas Island?
116. The statue of Eros in London's Piccadilly Circus is made from which material?
117. Who was the first actress to appear on a postage stamp?
118. What is the total number of dots on a standard die?
119. How many gallons in a bushel?
120. What is the fruit of the blackthorn tree known as?
121. Which high street bank uses the symbol of a black horse in its advertisements?
122. Who wrote the 'Aeneid'?
123. What is the occupation of a funambulist?
124. Which was the first year since the Second World War when there were two British general elections in the same year?
125. Which Oxford museum is the oldest in the world?
126. How many cubic feet in a cubic yard?
127. Which car company is known for manufacturing the 'Astra'?
128. Who wrote 'The Hitch-Hiker's Guide to the Galaxy'?
129. How many furlongs in a mile?
130. Which French fashion designer introduced the New Look?
131. Which French skier won three gold medals at the 1968 Winter Olympic Games?

132. In which country did the tango originate?

133. In which month is 'The Glorious Twelfth', the start of the grouse shooting season?

134. What is the smallest species of bat found in the British Isles?

135. What colour is the cross on the Swiss flag?

136. In which European country would you find regions called Umbria and Calabria?

137. What name is given to a young swan?

138. In which American city was John F. Kennedy assassinated?

139. By what name was Lesotho known until the 1960's?

140. What name is given to the branch of mathematics that deals with differentiation and integration?

141. In Greek mythology, who was the wife of Pluto?

142. Which sign of the zodiac is represented by a crab?

143. From which London terminus would you catch a train to Norwich?

144. In Greek mythology, who was the father of Zeus?

145. What is a Rhode Island Red?

146. In which city is the American version of 'Monopoly' set?

147. If all 50 of the United States of America were listed in alphabetical order, which would come first?

148. Walt Disney often provided the voice to which of his creations?

149. Which 1959 film won 11 Oscars?

150. Which country's secret service is called the Mossad?

151. Which number lies between 19 and 17 on a standard dartboard?

152. Launched in 1914, what was the name of the world's first aircraft carrier?

153. What is the longest river in the Republic of Ireland?

154. In which month is the vernal equinox?

155. In terms of area, which is the largest state in the U.S.A.?

156. Which of Snow White's seven dwarfs did not have a beard?

157. What was Buffalo Bill's real name?

158. Cars from which country bear the international vehicle

registration letters 'ZA'?

159. In 1921, on which Mediterranean island was Prince Philip, Duke of Edinburgh, born?

160. How high should the middle of a lawn tennis net be at the start of a game?

161. Which is Scotland's oldest university?

162. A leather wedding anniversary celebrates how many years of marriage?

163. Where was the liner, Queen Elizabeth, destroyed by fire in 1972?

164. In which American city is Logan International airport?

165. What was the name of Russia's first manned spacecraft?

166. Lutetia was the Roman name for which city?

167. Who was the first English monarch of the House of Saxe-Coburg?

168. Farsi is the official language of which country?

169. In contract bridge, how many tricks are needed to make a grand slam?

170. In which American state is Milwaukee?

171. Name *both* countries connected by the Simplon tunnel.

172. In which human organ would you find alveoli?

173. In which city was St. Peter martyred?

174. How many road-holding wheels had a Sinclair C5?

175. In which English county are Wookey Hole and Cheddar Gorge?

176. In which city would you find the Spanish Riding School?

177. What would a philatelist understand by the abbreviation 'F.D.C.'?

178. Which day of the week takes its name from the Anglo-Saxon god of war and the sky?

179. Which animal is the symbol of the Republican Party in the U.S.A.?

180. What would you be frightened of if you suffered from gametophobia?

181. On the fahrenheit scale, what is the boiling point of water?

182. Which is the oldest man-made structure on Earth visible from the moon?

183. Which British Royal House succeeded that of the House

of Saxe-Coburg and Gotha?

184. What is the sum of the internal angles of a hexagon?

185. What was the Christian name of the landscape gardener known as 'Capability' Brown?

186. Which English city was known to the Romans as Camulodunum?

187. If a circle has a diameter of 22 inches, what would be the length of its radius?

188. What name is given to the study of fossils?

189. In heraldry, a gryphon is half lion. Which animal makes up the other half?

190. In a motor car, what is mixed with petrol in the carburettor?

191. In the wager called a yankee, how many horses are selected?

192. Which poet wrote the words of the hymn 'Jerusalem'?

193. In which country are the French-speaking inhabitants called Walloons?

194. What does the musical term 'fortissimo' mean?

195. Which former capital city of Scotland stands on the River Tay?

196. What is the S.I. unit of electric current?

197. On whose poems was the musical 'Cats' based?

198. Which order of monks are known as the 'White Monks'?

199. What is the capital of Turkey?

200. Who sailed solo round the world in 1968 in a boat called 'Lively Lady'?

201. In which year did both Mother Teresa of Calcutta and Diana, Princess of Wales die?

202. What colour is the cross on the Danish flag?

203. On which river is the Kariba Dam?

204. Who is credited with inventing bifocal lenses and the lightning conductor?

205. Which Hindu deity's story is told in the 'Mahabharata', made into a multi-part TV series?

206. Which country's monarchs used to be crowned on Tara Hill?

207. Which racehorse won the British triple crown in 1970?

208. What would your poker hand be called if you held three sixes and two nines?
209. If you were suffering from ergophobia, of what would you be afraid?
210. In which British city would you find 'Arthur's Seat'?
211. On which English lake did Donald Campbell meet his death?
212. What colour is the neutral wire on a modern British domestic plug?
213. Which comic book hero, created by Frank Hampson, appeared in the 'Eagle'?
214. The former county of Rutland became a part of which other county in 1974?
215. Whose real name was Vladimir Ilyich Ulyanov?
216. Who was German Minister for Enlightenment and Propaganda from 1933–45?
217. Which day of the week do the French call 'samedi'?
218. Who was the first astronaut to walk in space?
219. Who was the first man to win the Wimbledon Men's Singles title three years in succession after World War II?
220. When was Desert Orchid's birthday?
221. In which country was John Calvin born?
222. Who was the last Tsar of Russia?
223. In the nursery rhyme, what did Little Jack Horner pull out with his thumb?
224. In which English county did the Great Train Robbery take place?
225. Which famous murderer lived at Ten Rillington Place?
226. Who assassinated Robert Kennedy?
227. Who was the god of love in Greek mythology?
228. What is scotopic vision better known as?
229. In pre-decimal coinage, how many 'tanners' were there in 'ten bob'?
230. From what part of the plant is liquorice obtained?
231. Who is the Patron Saint of France?
232. Who wrote the political treatise 'The Rights of Man'?
233. In economics, what do the letters 'PSBR' stand for?
234. Who was the leader of the religious group the Lollards?

235. How many players are there in a volleyball team?

236. What was the original name of Drake's ship 'The Golden Hind'?

237. The liver of which animal is used to make paté de foie gras?

238. What did Winston Churchill refer to in 1939 as 'a riddle wrapped in a mystery inside an enigma'?

239. If you are suffering from panphobia or pantophobia, of what would you be afraid?

240. Which gulf separates Sweden and Finland?

241. How many hoops are used in a game of croquet?

242. Which disease is transmitted by the tsetse fly?

243. Which dukedom is in the Howard family?

244. In the USA, how many nickels make one dollar?

245. What is the points value of the yellow ball in a game of snooker?

246. What was the name of the ship that was meant to accompany the Mayflower taking the Pilgrim Fathers to America?

247. What is the lowest score impossible to obtain on a standard dartboard with a single dart?

248. How many children were there in Enid Blyton's 'Famous Five'?

249. On a standard map of the London Underground, what colour is the Central Line?

250. Which Parliamentary post has been held by Horace King, Selwyn Lloyd, George Thomas and Bernard Weatherill?

251. Which daily newspaper is known as the 'Thunderer'?

252. Which Saint's Day is celebrated on November 30th?

253. What colour was Britain's first twopenny postage stamp?

254. What kind of animal is a phalarope?

255. Which scientist first prepared sodium?

256. Around which planet do the moons Titan, Hyperion and Phoebe orbit?

257. In which county is the Prime Ministerial residence 'Chequers'?

258. The Holger Nielson and the Revised Sylvester are both methods of what?

259. Who discovered the circulation of the blood?

260. What is a male bee known as?

261. Which human organ is affected by Bright's Disease?

262. Which is the only even prime number?

263. What was the first American city to host the Summer Olympic Games?

264. What type of plant is attacked by the Boll Weevil?

265. What is the more popular name given to Nitrous Oxide?

266. Which American city is known as the City of Brotherly Love?

267. In which city is the Jacques Cartier Bridge?

268. In pre-decimal coinage, how many farthings made up a half-crown?

269. For which discovery were Sir Frederick Banting and J.J.R. Macleod awarded Nobel Prizes in 1923?

270. What nationality was the navigator after whom the Barents Sea is named?

271. During whose reign was Thomas A Becket murdered?

272. By what name is Edward Teach, who died in 1718, better known?

273. Who was sheriff of Lincoln County in 1881?

274. What nationality was Robert Bunsen, the inventor of the bunsen burner?

275. Who was the youngest son of Prince Andrew of Greece and Princess Alice of Battenburg?

276. Which shipping forecast area lies due north of Dogger?

277. In which city did Diana, Princess of Wales die?

278. By what name is the former territory of Northern Rhodesia now known?

279. Who was the first Secretary-General of the United Nations?

280. Other than Troilus and Cressida, name either of the other two Shakespearian plays with a woman's name in the title.

281. Which car manufacturer made models called the 'Esprit', the 'Eclat' and the 'Excel'?

282. In which city did the robbery take place in the 1969 film 'The Italian Job'?

283. Developed in the 1950's, the Salk vaccine is a protection

against which disease?

284. How many stars appear on the U.S. flag?

285. Which famous club was founded by Sir Francis Dashwood in 1755?

286. Who played the part of Edmund Blackadder on television?

287. To which country does Easter Island belong?

288. What would you expect a sommelier to serve you with?

289. Who was the first of the Beatles to have a solo UK number one hit single?

290. By what name is the crane-fly usually called?

291. In the nursery rhyme which begins 'Mary, Mary, quite contrary . . .', what were 'all in a row'?

292. Which organisation produces the publication, the 'War Cry'?

293. Which is the longest bone in the human body?

294. What was the name of the first re-usable space craft?

295. For which film were the names of seven leading characters chosen after a public opinion poll?

296. With which pop group would you associate Peter Tork and Michael Nesmith?

297. What term is given to −273.15 degrees centigrade?

298. How many incisor teeth would a normal adult expect to have?

299. The rules of which Olympic sport were drawn up by Teddington H.C. in 1871?

300. Of what disease did Prince Albert die in 1861?

Films Quick Questions (*Answers on page 177*)

1. Which rock star played the title role in the 1970 film 'Ned Kelly'?

2. In which series of films have Bob Monkhouse, Phil Silvers, Dora Bryan and Frankie Howerd all appeared?

3. Which 1945 film directed by David Lean and adapted from the one-act Noel Coward play 'Still Life', used music from Rachmaninoff's Second Piano Concerto?

4. Whose directorial debut was the 1969 film 'Oh! What a Lovely War'?

5. On which island was the actor Errol Flynn born?

6. What was the name of the motel featured in Alfred Hitchcock's film 'Psycho'?

7. Which actor played the father of Indiana Jones in the 'Last Crusade'?

8. In 'The Bridge on the River Kwai', which actor commanded the force that was sent to destroy the bridge?

9. Which 1984 film was based on the memoirs of the New York Times reporter Sydney Schanberg?

10. Which historical character did Errol Flynn play in the 1941 film 'They Died With Their Boots On'?

11. Who played the part of Sir James Bond in the 1967 film 'Casino Royale'?

12. In 'The Sound of Music', how many children comprised the Von Trapp family?

13. Who played Hercule Poirot in the 1974 film 'Murder on the Orient Express'?

14. Which was the last of the series of 'Road to . . .' films starring Bob Hope and Bing Crosby?

15. Who played the title role in the 1965 film 'Doctor Zhivago'?

16. Which rock group performed the score for the 1980 film 'Flash Gordon'?

17. Which actor played the part of Doctor Who in two films in the 1960's?

18. Which actor played the Prime Minister of Freedonia, Rufus T. Firefly, in a 1933 film?

19. Which famous French film director played the part of a scientist in the film 'Close Encounters of the Third Kind'?

20. Who played the part of Sam Spade in the 1941 film 'The Maltese Falcon'?

21. Which 1939 film starred a character called Dorothy and her dog, Toto?

22. Which actress starred in 'Anna Christie' in 1930, and 'Anna Karenina' in 1935?

23. In which Walt Disney classic would you find the three fairies Flora, Fauna and Merryweather?

24. Which British comedian played the part of a sheriff in the

1985 western 'Silverado'?

25. Which actor played the title role in 'The Absent-Minded Professor'?

26. For which film was Peter Finch awarded an Oscar posthumously?

27. What was the name of the character played by Liza Minnelli in the film 'Cabaret'?

28. Who played the part of Captain Queeg in the 1954 film 'The Caine Mutiny'?

29. Which 1983 James Bond film was a remake of 'Thunderball'?

30. What was the title of the million selling record first sung in the 1942 film 'Holiday Inn'?

31. Which actress played the title role in the 1983 film 'Educating Rita'?

32. Who sang the song 'As Time Goes By' in the 1942 film 'Casablanca'?

33. Who played the title role in the 1965 film 'Cat Ballou'?

34. Which real-life jockey was portrayed by John Hurt in the film 'Champions'?

35. Which 1981 film, which won an Academy Award for best picture, was based around the 1924 Olympics and the events leading up to it?

36. What was the title of the 1958 film starring Kenneth More and David McCallum based on the sinking of the Titanic?

37. What was the title of the 1979 film starring Jane Fonda and Michael Douglas about the attempted cover-up of an accident at a nuclear plant?

38. Which actor won the final hand of poker in the 1965 film 'The Cincinnati Kid'?

39. The works of which classical composer were most widely used in Stanley Kubrick's 'A Clockwork Orange'?

40. Who directed the films 'Comfort and Joy', 'Local Hero' and 'Gregory's Girl'?

41. Which musical, and film, was based on the H.G. Wells novel 'Kipps'?

42. The 1980 film 'Coal Miner's Daughter' starring Sissy Spacek was based on the life of which country singer?

43. What single word was written on Citizen Kane's sledge?
44. Who directed the films '1941' and 'The Color Purple'?
45. What was the title of the 1987 film, directed by David Attenborough, based on the life (and death) of the South African, Steve Biko?
46. Which 1969 film starring Barbra Streisand was based on Thornton Wilder's 'The Matchmaker'?
47. In the 1969 film 'The Love Bug', what make of car was Herbie?
48. Which actor won an Oscar for his performance as the sheriff in the 1952 film 'High Noon'?
49. Which actress played the shared wife of Lee Marvin and Clint Eastwood in the film 'Paint Your Wagon'?
50. Which 1941 film, regarding a family of Welsh coal miners, directed by John Ford and starring Walter Pidgeon and Maureen O'Hara, won five Oscars, including Best Picture?
51. Which film, based on the novel by George Orwell, marked Richard Burton's final performance?
52. The film 'Nevada Smith' starring Steve McQueen was based on a character from which novel?
53. Which game was Paul Newman's source of income in the 1961 film 'The Hustler'?
54. Which actor made his directorial debut in the 1978 film 'Paradise Alley'?
55. What was the sequel to the film 'Gentlemen Prefer Blondes'?
56. Portrayed by Meryl Streep in the film 'Out of Africa', what was the nationality of Karen Blixen?
57. What was the surname of the father and daughter who starred in the 1973 film 'Paper Moon'?
58. What type of business was carried out in the premises of '84 Charing Cross Road'?
59. Which 1985 film starring Michael Douglas and Kathleen Turner was a sequel to the film 'Romancing the Stone'?
60. Which 1973 film shows Steve McQueen attempting to escape from Devil's Island?
61. Which 1962 film starring John Wayne, Henry Fonda and Robert Mitchum was based on Operation Overlord?

62. What was the title of the 1949 comedy, starring Stanley Holloway and Margaret Rutherford, in which an ancient treaty is discovered allowing independence for a part of London?

63. Which wild west duo were played on film, and on television, by Clayton Moore and Jay Silverheels?

64. Who directed the 1973 film 'Pat Garrett and Billy the Kid' which starred Kris Kristofferson, with a musical score from Bob Dylan?

65. In which Chinese city was the 1987 film 'Empire of the Sun' set?

66. Who played the title role in the 1986 film 'Peggy Sue Got Married'?

67. Who played the title role in the 1968 musical 'Oliver!'?

68. Who played the part of Elizabeth I in the 1939 film 'The Private Lives of Elizabeth and Essex'?

69. Which American comedian played the part of a sheet music salesman in the 1981 film 'Pennies From Heaven', based on Dennis Potter's television mini-series?

70. Who played the part of James Bond in the 1969 film 'On Her Majesty's Secret Service'?

71. Which political cartoonist contributed some animated sequences for the 1982 film 'Pink Floyd – The Wall'?

72. Which actor played the part of Al Capone in the 1987 film 'The Untouchables'?

73. In which 1951 film does Humphrey Bogart play the part of Charlie Allnutt?

74. Which ex-Monty Python star appeared in the 1985 film 'A Private Function'?

75. Who played the title role in the 1971 film 'One Day in the Life of Ivan Denisovich'?

76. Which 1946 film starring Lana Turner and John Garfield was remade in 1981 starring Jack Nicholson and Jessica Lange?

77. Which former sports journalist's last film role was in 'The Killers' in 1964?

78. Which film marked Timothy Dalton's debut as James Bond?

79. The 1985 Kurosawa-directed film 'Ran' is an adaptation of which Shakespearian play?

80. The 1987 film 'Personal Services' was based on whose real life story?

81. In the 1966 film 'Khartoum', Charlton Heston played the part of General Gordon. Which famous actor played the part of the Mahdi?

82. Which 1957 romantic comedy starring Laurence Olivier and Marilyn Monroe was based on Terence Rattigan's play 'The Sleeping Prince'?

83. Which film involved John Mills, Sylvia Sims and Anthony Quayle being stranded behind enemy lines during World War 2?

84. Which 1948 John Huston-directed film, also starring Humphrey Bogart and Lauren Bacall, starred Edward G. Robinson as a gangster holding the residents of a Florida hotel captive during a particularly severe storm?

85. In which 1986 film did David Bowie star as the King of the Goblins?

86. Which 1955 film, Disney's first in Cinemascope, featured the voice of Peggy Lee as a Siamese cat?

87. In which 1968 film did Steve McQueen play chess with Faye Dunaway?

88. In which 1962 film did Bette Davis and Joan Crawford star as two ageing sisters, both ex-actresses?

89. In which 1985 film was Harrison Ford cast as a policeman hiding out with the American Amish community?

90. Who starred as Joe Lampton in the 1959 film 'Room at the Top'?

91. Which was the only Bob Hope/Bing Crosby 'Road' film to be made in colour?

92. Which film hero has been played by Elmo Lincoln, Buster Crabbe, Lex Barker and Christopher Lambert?

93. Who played the part of a schoolteacher in the 1970 film 'Ryan's Daughter'?

94. Which couple were played by Warren Beatty and Faye Dunaway in a 1967 film?

95. Which actor played the part of Danny De Vito's twin

brother in the 1988 film 'Twins'?

96. Played by Miranda Richardson in the 1985 film 'Dance With a Stranger', who was the last woman to have been hanged in Britain?

97. What was the name of the character played by Judy Garland in 'The Wizard of Oz'?

98. In which famous 1949 film did James Cagney star as a psychopath with an obsession about his mother?

99. Who played the part of Father O'Malley in the 1940's films 'Going My Way' and 'The Bells of St. Mary's'?

100. Which comedy duo's first film was 'Morons From Outer Space'?

Geography Quick Questions (*Answers on page 178*)

1. Which country is home to the airline Iberia?
2. Of which country is Windhoek the capital?
3. Which town lies at the northern end of the Suez Canal?
4. In terms of population, what is the largest city on South Island, New Zealand?
5. The most northerly point on the continent of Africa lies in which country?
6. What is the capital of Thailand?
7. Which British port has four tides a day?
8. In which ocean are the Seychelles?
9. Name *both* the islands separated by the Cook Strait.
10. Which country is bordered by Panama and Nicaragua?
11. Which range of mountains separates France from Spain?
12. In which country is the highest peak on the continent of Africa?
13. Which river forms much of the boundary between Norfolk and Suffolk?
14. Off the coast of which country would you find the Gulf of Carpentaria?
15. What is the longest river in Europe?
16. In which country is the source of the River Danube?
17. Which country is home to Varig Airlines?
18. Which of the Great Lakes in North America is the largest?
19. What is the name of the deepest part of the Pacific Ocean?

20. Which Irish county stretches the furthest north?
21. Which European country colonized Angola and Mozambique?
22. Quito is the capital of which country?
23. Which river flows through Moscow?
24. In which country does the River Rhine flow into the sea?
25. In which country is the highest peak in the Alps?
26. Into what stretch of water does the Danube flow?
27. What is the State Capital of New York?
28. Which country has the International Vehicle Registration Letter 'C'?
29. In which American city would you find La Guardia airport?
30. In terms of area, which is the largest Australian State?
31. In which English county are the Quantock Hills?
32. In terms of population, what is the largest city in West Yorkshire?
33. Of which country is Valletta the capital?
34. In which country is there a mountain range called the Southern Alps?
35. Which is the only South American country where Portuguese is the official language?
36. In which country is the confluence of the Blue and White Niles?
37. Name the highest peak in the U.S.A.
38. What is denoted by '0' on the Beaufort Scale?
39. In which country is Lake Balaton?
40. In which county are England's ten highest peaks?
41. What is Bechuanaland now known as?
42. In which English county is Harwich?
43. What is the capital city of Nicaragua?
44. In which country is the world's highest waterfall, Angel Falls?
45. Which republic, the smallest in the world, is entirely surrounded by the Italian region Emilia-Romagna?
46. On which river is the Hoover Dam?
47. In which European city are the headquarters of O.P.E.C.?
48. In which city would you find the 'Spanish Steps'?

49. On which river are the Victoria Falls?
50. Which sea separates New Zealand from Australia?
51. In which country would you find Mount Cotopaxi?
52. What is the capital city of Peru?
53. What is the official language of Liechtenstein?
54. LOT is the national airline of which country?
55. What is the second-longest river in Africa?
56. Which is the world's largest freshwater lake?
57. To which country do the Galapagos Islands belong?
58. In which country is the port of Dar Es Salaam?
59. Which country is surrounded by the Pacific Ocean, the South China Sea, the Sulu Sea and the Celebes Sea?
60. What is the capital of Pakistan?
61. Which desert of around 400,000 square miles covers much of Mongolia?
62. What is the capital of Estonia?
63. India, Bangladesh and Burma all border onto which bay?
64. What is the largest British city on the River Lagan?
65. Which canal of just over 50 miles in length was opened in 1914?
66. In which country is the world's longest vehicular tunnel?
67. In meteorology, what name is given to an area of high atmospheric pressure?
68. In which desert was no rainfall recorded for over 350 years until 1971?
69. Of which African country is Freetown the capital?
70. Which Scandinavian country extends the furthest north?
71. In which South American country is the town of Fray Bentos?
72. The Gulf of California is surrounded by which country?
73. Which U.S. state extends the furthest east?
74. In terms of area, which is the largest country on the continent of Africa?
75. What was the former name of Harare, the capital of Zimbabwe?
76. Which river forms much of the border between Devon and Cornwall?
77. What is the capital of Haiti?

78. Which is the only U.S. state which is south of the Tropic of Cancer?
79. In which island group is Scapa Flow?
80. What is the name given to a hundredth part of a shekel in Israel?
81. Which U.S. city is served by the John F. Kennedy International airport?
82. Which is the most southerly of the Welsh counties?
83. Which of the four main islands of Japan lies furthest north?
84. Cars from which country bear the International Vehicle Registration letter 'S'?
85. Off the coast of which Australian state is Kangaroo Island?
86. In which country in the Middle East would you find the towns of Mosul and Kirkuk?
87. Which island group are known as 'The Friendly Islands'?
88. In which country would you find the Vosges mountains?
89. Papua New Guinea is separated from which country by the Torres Strait?
90. In which bay would you find Southampton Island?
91. In which ocean is the island of Tristan Da Cunha?
92. Which is the most northerly county in England?
93. In which English county is Sizewell?
94. What was the former name of Maputo, the capital of Mozambique?
95. In which country would you find Lake Vanern?
96. Cars from which country would bear the International Vehicle Registration letters 'EAK'?
97. Which is the most widely spoken language in Switzerland?
98. What is the capital of Barbados?
99. In terms of population, what is the largest city in Brazil?
100. How many counties are there in Wales?

History Quick Questions (*Answers on page 180*)
1. Who was the last British monarch from the House of York?
2. Who was United States President from 1953 to 1961?

3. In which city was Joan of Arc burnt to death for being a witch?

4. Which Chinese leader established Peking as their winter capital?

5. During which single military action were the most V.C.'s won?

6. Which Irish missionary and saint founded a monastery on the island of Iona?

7. Who was King of England at the time of the Gunpowder plot?

8. Who was assassinated by James Earl Ray?

9. Who was British Prime Minister when Old Age Pensions were first introduced?

10. Which war was ended by the Treaty of Portsmouth in 1905?

11. Which Cabinet post did Winston Churchill hold between 1924 and 1929?

12. 1712 saw the last execution in England for which crime?

13. The ideas of which famous astronomer was Galileo warned by the Inquisition to stop teaching?

14. Who was the first British monarch to be styled 'Defender of the Faith'?

15. Which political leader was assassinated by John Wilkes Booth?

16. Who succeeded Charles de Gaulle as French President in 1969?

17. Which of the five permanent members of the United Nations Security Council was never a member of the League of Nations?

18. What relation was Napoleon III to Napoleon Bonaparte?

19. Who was British Prime Minister on V.J. Day?

20. Which battle saw the final defeat of the Jacobites in 1746?

21. The 18th Amendment introduced Prohibition in the United States, but which amendment abolished it?

22. At which castle did the investiture of the Prince of Wales take place in 1969?

23. Who was the last British monarch to be born outside the British Isles?

24. How many times did Mary Queen of Scots get married?

25. Who commanded the British forces that captured Quebec from the French in 1759?

26. In which country is the site of the battle of Waterloo?

27. Name Oliver Cromwell's successor as Lord Protector.

28. Which British monarch was the great-grandfather of Queen Elizabeth II?

29. Of which American Indian tribe was Sitting Bull a member?

30. Who was the last British Chancellor of the Exchequer whose father had held the same post?

31. Who was First Secretary of the Czechoslovak Communist Party at the time of the Russian invasion in 1968?

32. Which Crown Colony was ceded to Britain by the Treaty of Utrecht in 1713?

33. Who was the last British monarch to be born in Scotland?

34. Which *two* states fought the Punic Wars?

35. On which small island did the USA first test their hydrogen bomb in 1954?

36. In which city was the first skyscraper built in 1883?

37. Of which country was Hastings Banda the first Prime Minister?

38. Who was German Chancellor at the time of the signing of unconditional surrender on 7th May 1945?

39. Which German battleship was scuttled in 1939 after the battle of the River Plate?

40. Which country invaded Abyssinia in 1935?

41. What was the name of the first wooden steamship to cross the Atlantic?

42. Who was the first *Democrat* U.S. President to be assassinated?

43. Which Pope died barely a month after election in 1978?

44. In which century did the Black Death kill up to half the British population?

45. Who was elected President of the American Confederacy?

46. In which country was Simon Bolivar born?

47. Which Spaniard led the conquest of Peru in 1532?

48. Of which tribe was Boadicea the queen?

49. Which famous battle took place on Senlac Hill?
50. The planned invasion of which country was codenamed 'Operation Sealion' during World War II?
51. Which British Cabinet post has been held by the Earls of Wilmington, Bute, Chatham and Shelburne?
52. Who invented the Spinning Jenny?
53. Who commanded the victorious British forces at the battles of Blenheim, Ramillies, Oudenaarde and Malplaquet?
54. Who was the husband of Marie Antoinette?
55. Which British general led the winning army in the Battle of Plassey in 1757?
56. Which grandson of Genghis Khan founded the Yuan dynasty in China?
57. Who was the last Viceroy of India?
58. Who was President of the U.S.A. throughout World War I?
59. How many soldiers made up a Roman cohort?
60. Which Nazi was German Ambassador to Britain from 1936–1938, Foreign Minister from 1938–1945 and was hanged in 1946 after being found guilty of war crimes at Nuremburg?
61. With which country would you associate the statesman Syngman Rhee?
62. Who succeeded the Empress Zaudita in 1930 and during his reign was twice deposed; once by the Italians and later by a military coup?
63. After which explorer is America named?
64. During which war was the gatling gun first used?
65. In 1346 during the Hundred Years War, what was the name of the battle in which Edward III's English army defeated a much larger army led by King Philip?
66. What became the capital of the Roman empire in 330 A.D. when Rome was abandoned?
67. Which English agriculturalist introduced the horse-drawn hoe and the seed-drill?
68. What was the name of the English physicist who discovered the electron and was winner of the Nobel Prize for

Physics in 1906?

69. Which Greek physician has been called the 'Father of Medicine'?

70. With which historical figure would you associate Clara Petacci?

71. Who designed the first lightning conductor?

72. Which fifteenth century military leader was canonized in 1920?

73. Who was the first woman to fly solo from England to Australia?

74. Which winner of the Nobel Peace Prize was assassinated by Muslim fundamentalists in 1981?

75. In which European capital city were approximately 30,000 people killed in an earthquake in 1755?

76. Which country did the Prussians defeat at the battle of Sadowa in 1866?

77. Which islands were discovered by John Davis in 1592?

78. Who was the last Saxon King of England?

79. Of which kingdom was Offa the king?

80. On which island was Captain James Cook killed in 1779?

81. Who invented the Spinning Mule in 1779?

82. Who founded the Salvation Army?

83. In 1917, what became the first item ever to be rationed in Great Britain?

84. Which British Prime Minister became the First Earl of Dwyfor?

85. What was the name of the Spartan King who unsuccessfully attempted to halt Xerxes' Persians at the pass of Thermopylae with his 300 soldiers?

86. In which city was Trotsky murdered in 1940?

87. What aid to motoring was invented by Percy Shaw in 1934?

88. Who was the Aztec Emperor of Mexico at the time of the Spanish conquest?

89. Which religious order was founded by St. Ignatius Loyola?

90. Who was the first British Prime Minister to have been born in the twentieth century?

91.   In which British city did the Peterloo Massacre take place in 1819?

92.   Which city was excavated by the archaeologist Heinrich Schliemann from 1870?

93.   Of which country was Alexander Kerensky the Prime Minister in 1917?

94.   Which musical instrument was invented by Cristofori in the early eighteenth century?

95.   Which statesman fought against the British in one war, but later became a member of the British Cabinet during another war?

96.   By what nickname is the political leader François Duvalier better remembered?

97.   Who was English king at the end of the Hundred Years War?

98.   At which battle of 1685 was the pretender to the British throne, the Duke of Monmouth, defeated?

99.   What was the name of the naval battle at which Octavius defeated Anthony and Cleopatra?

100. Which architect remodelled the Brighton Pavilion for the Prince Regent?

Literature Quick Questions (*Answers on page 181*)

1.   What was the name of Sherlock Holmes' brother?

2.   Which author wrote the play 'Toad of Toad Hall'?

3.   Which English novelist wrote 'The Loved One' and 'Vile Bodies'?

4.   What was the name of the shrew in Shakespeare's 'The Taming of the Shrew'?

5.   Which book, published in 1719, was based on the true-life experiences of Alexander Selkirk?

6.   Who created the fictional land of Narnia?

7.   Who wrote the children's adventure 'Swallows and Amazons'?

8.   Which science fiction writer wrote the 'Foundation' trilogy?

9.   In the Sherlock Holmes stories what was Doctor Watson's first name?

10. Lydia Languish appears as the heroine in which of Sheridan's plays?

11. Who was the author of the novels 'The French Lieutenant's Woman' and 'The Magus'?

12. Who wrote the play 'Tamburlaine The Great'?

13. In which novel does Becky Sharp appear?

14. Which word was first introduced into the English language in a 1920 play called 'R.U.R.' by the Czech novelist Karel Capek?

15. Name *both* courtiers who served the king in Shakespeare's 'Hamlet' who also appear in the title of the play by Tom Stoppard.

16. In which J.D. Salinger novel is the central character called Holden Caulfield?

17. Which pseudonym was used by the writer Hector Hugh Munro?

18. Which detective features in the stories 'The Nine Tailors' and 'Murder Must Advertise'?

19. Which playwright wrote 'Equus', 'Amadeus' and 'The Royal Hunt of the Sun'?

20. Who wrote the poems 'The Rape of Lucrece' and 'Venus and Adonis'?

21. What was the name of the dog in Enid Blyton's Famous Five stories?

22. Who wrote the play which was later turned into the musical 'My Fair Lady'?

23. Who wrote the plays 'School for Scandal' and 'The Rivals'?

24. Who wrote the books 'The Loneliness of the Long Distance Runner' and 'Saturday Night and Sunday Morning'?

25. Under what name did J.B. Morton write his regular column in the Daily Express from 1924–1975?

26. Which British politician wrote the novels 'Coningsby', 'Sybil' and 'Tancred'?

27. How many lines are there in a sonnet?

28. Which fictional detective first appeared in the book 'The Mysterious Affair at Styles' in 1920?

29. Who wrote the book 'Peter Pan'?

30. By what name is the writer of adventure stories, Lord Tweedsmuir, better remembered?

31. In Emily Brontë's 'Wuthering Heights', what was the name of the waif adopted by the Earnshaw family?

32. Which comedian wrote the books 'Adolf Hitler – My Part in His Downfall' and 'Mussolini – His Part in My Downfall'?

33. Which famous work is set in the Welsh town of Llareggub and features the characters Polly Garter, Captain Cat and Myfanwy Price?

34. Which novel by James Joyce deals with the events of one day, 16 June 1904, in Dublin?

35. Who wrote the stories 'The Picture of Dorian Gray' and 'Lord Arthur Savile's Crime'?

36. How many lines are there in a limerick?

37. To which London landmark was Wordsworth referring in his line 'Earth has not anything to show more fair'?

38. In Coleridge's 'Kubla Khan', where was there to be a 'stately pleasure-dome'?

39. Who wrote the books 'The Day of the Triffids', 'The Midwich Cuckoos' and 'The Chrysalids'?

40. Which former M.P. wrote the novels 'Not a Penny More, Not a Penny Less', and 'First Among Equals'?

41. Mrs. Doasyouwouldbedoneby and Mrs. Bedonebyasyoudid appear in which novel by Charles Kingsley?

42. Who wrote the play 'Waiting for Godot'?

43. Who wrote the books 'Squirrel Nutkin' and 'The Tale of Peter Rabbit'?

44. Who wrote the books 'Burmese Days' and 'Keep the Aspidistra Flying'?

45. 'Five Children and It', 'The Phoenix and the Carpet' and 'The Railway Children' were written by which children's author?

46. In Coleridge's poem 'The Rime of the Ancient Mariner', what type of bird was hung round the mariner's neck?

47. Who is the narrator in R.L. Stevenson's book 'Treasure Island'?

48. Who wrote the children's book 'The Secret Garden'?

49. Later made into TV mini-series, who wrote the books 'Porterhouse Blue' and 'Blott on the Landscape'?

50. According to Sue Townsend, how old was Adrian Mole when he first started writing his 'Secret Diary'?

51. 'Crockford's' is a reference book relating to which particular group of people?

52. What was the name of the cottage on the shores of Lake Grasmere in the Lake District in which William Wordsworth lived?

53. In 'Gulliver's Travels', what is the name of the land of the giants?

54. What nationality were the father and son writers of the series of guide books, Karl and Fritz Baedeker?

55. Who was the author of 'The Darling Buds of May', made into a TV series in the 1990's?

56. In which novel by Thomas Hardy does the character Bathsheba Everdene appear?

57. In Chaucer's 'Canterbury Tales', how many 'tales' are told?

58. Who wrote the novel 'The Strange Case of Dr. Jekyll and Mr Hyde'?

59. In which of Oscar Wilde's plays do the characters Lady Bracknell, Miss Prism and Algy all appear?

60. In 'The Song of Hiawatha' by Longfellow, what was the name of Hiawatha's wife?

61. On which island was the writer V.S. Naipaul born?

62. In which of Shakespeare's plays does the jester, Feste, appear?

63. What pseudonym did Charles Dickens use for his contributions to the Morning Chronicle?

64. Who wrote the novel 'Lorna Doone'?

65. Which nineteenth century author created the characters 'Archdeacon Grantly', 'Dr. Proudie' and 'Mr. Quiverful'?

66. In George Bernard Shaw's 'Major Barbara', of which army was the Major a member?

67. Who wrote the novels 'Adam Bede', 'Middlemarch' and 'Silas Marner'?

68. Which poet wrote odes to 'A Grecian Urn', 'Autumn' and

'A Nightingale'?

69. Which American novelist wrote 'The Naked and the Dead'?

70. In which of Shakespeare's plays does the slave, Caliban, appear?

71. Which of the so-called 'angry young men' wrote the play 'Look Back In Anger'?

72. In which of Dickens' novels does the Gradgrind family appear?

73. Which publishing company was formed by Allen Lane in 1936?

74. Which vicar and lecturer in mathematics wrote the book 'The Hunting of the Snark'?

75. What was the name of William Shakespeare's wife?

76. In which of Jane Austen's novels does the Bennet family appear?

77. Who wrote the novel 'A Clockwork Orange'?

78. Which Canadian singer/songwriter wrote the novels 'Beautiful Losers' and 'The Favourite Game'?

79. What was the name of the Brontë sisters' brother?

80. Although best remembered for his war poems, who wrote the semi-autobiographical novel 'Memoirs of a Fox-Hunting Man'?

81. Later made into a TV series and film, who wrote 'The Singing Detective'?

82. On which First World War poet's works did Benjamin Britten base his 'War Requiem'?

83. Who wrote four novels known collectively as the 'Raj Quartet' on which the TV series 'The Jewel in the Crown' was based?

84. What was the name of Don Quixote's servant?

85. Who wrote the novels 'A Town Like Alice' and 'On The Beach', both later made into films?

86. In Shakespeare's 'Romeo and Juliet', what was the surname of Juliet?

87. Who wrote the novels 'I, Claudius' and 'Claudius the God'?

88. Until abolished in 1962, which officer had the responsibility

for licensing plays?

89. Which author created the flying ace Biggles?

90. What was the middle name of the poet Shelley?

91. Who wrote the play 'Murder in the Cathedral' about the murder of Thomas A Becket?

92. In 'Treasure Island' what was the name of Long John Silver's parrot?

93. Which fictional secret agent first appeared in the book 'Call For The Dead' in 1961?

94. 'Rupert of Hentzau' was the sequel to which of Anthony Hope's novels?

95. Who was the first person to be officially given the title 'Poet Laureate'?

96. In 'Treasure Island', what was the name of the inn kept by Jim Hawkins' mother?

97. Which Russian author wrote 'The Idiot', 'Crime and Punishment' and 'The Brothers Karamazov'?

98. Which writer created the fictional hero Tarzan?

99. What is the surname of the brother and sister who wrote 'Tales From Shakespeare'?

100. What is the name of Othello's wife in the Shakespeare play?

Music Quick Questions (*Answers on page 182*)

1. Which group's first UK hit single was 'New York Mining Disaster 1941', released in 1967?

2. Which of the four Beatles had solo UK top ten hits in the 1970's with 'It Don't Come Easy' and 'Back Off Boogaloo'?

3. What was the previous name of the English National Opera?

4. The Polonaise is a dance from which country?

5. With which musical instrument would you associate Larry Adler?

6. Which *two* planets are absent from Holst's 'Planet Suite'?

7. What was the name of Billy J. Kramer's backing band?

8. Who was Elvis Presley's manager?

9. Who wrote the ballets 'The Firebird', 'Petrushka' and 'The Rite of Spring'?

10. Whom did Ronnie Wood replace as a member of the Rolling Stones?

11. What nationality was the composer Georges Bizet?

12. Who were Wayne Fontana's backing group?

13. Who wrote 'Orpheus in the Underworld' and 'Tales of Hoffman'?

14. What nationality was the composer Hector Berlioz?

15. Which act appeared live at both the British and American 1985 Live Aid concerts at Wembley and Philadelphia?

16. Which term is used to describe singing unaccompanied by any musical instrument, or more literally 'in the chapel style'?

17. Who composed the music for the film 'Zorba the Greek'?

18. 'Go Now' was the only UK number one hit single for which group?

19. Who, in opera, was the knight who sought the Holy Grail?

20. What nickname is given to Beethoven's last piano concerto, No. 5 in E flat, Opus 73?

21. Which successful solo artiste has also had UK top ten hits with Queen, Mick Jagger and Bing Crosby?

22. Who composed the opera 'Peter Grimes'?

23. Which successful American group were once known as Carl and the Passions?

24. Which female voice lies between contralto and soprano?

25. With which pop group would you associate Stuart Sutcliffe and Pete Best?

26. Which singer, the subject of a hit musical, was played by Timothy Whitnall, Shakin' Stevens and P.J. Proby, each representing different stages in his career?

27. Which American jazz pianist and composer who died in 1974 was christened with the forenames Edward Kennedy?

28. Who was the first Canadian singer to have a UK number one hit, with the song 'Diana'?

29. Who wrote the operas 'Turandot' and 'Madam Butterfly'?

30. Which track was the double A-side with 'Strawberry Fields Forever' by the Beatles?

31. Which opera by Verdi was commissioned by the Khedive of Egypt?

32. Which pop group took their name from two characters from 'The Adventures of Tintin' by Hergé?

33. In which English county is the Glyndebourne Opera House?

34. Which record by Slade has re-entered the charts virtually every year since it was first released in 1973?

35. Which Italian word means slow, or dignified in style?

36. Which rock group has released albums called 'Exile on Main Street', 'Sticky Fingers' and 'Goats Head Soup'?

37. What is the surname of the man who had a UK Top Ten hit in 1968, ten years after his mother had acheived the same feat?

38. Who composed the operas 'Don Giovanni' and 'Cosi Fan Tutte', and the Jupiter Symphony?

39. In which musical instrument would you find 'stickers', 'pallets' and a 'windchest'?

40. Who had a hit in 1971 with the theme music from the film 'Shaft'?

41. In which film based on a rock opera by Pete Townshend of The Who, did Sting appear as a bellboy?

42. Which Italian, the son of an innkeeper, wrote three operas based on works by Shakespeare?

43. What was the first name of George Gershwin's elder brother who often wrote the words for his musicals?

44. Who had a UK number one hit with 'The Ballad of Bonnie and Clyde'?

45. What is the name of the opera house which is part of New York's Lincoln Center for the Performing Arts?

46. Which actress teamed up with Peter Sellers to release two UK hit singles in the early 1960's?

47. Which British group had three UK Top Ten hits in the 1960's with songs written by Bob Dylan?

48. Who composed six Brandenburg Concertos?

49. What was the name of Johnny Johnson's backing group?

50. Cliff Richard featured on two UK number one hits with the same title almost 27 years apart. What was it called?

Radio and Television Quick Questions (*Answers on page 183*)

1. Whose secretary was Della Street?
2. In which fictional town is Coronation Street set?
3. Who took over from Roy Plomley on 'Desert Island Discs'?
4. On which British TV series was the American series 'All in the Family' based?
5. In which village does Postman Pat deliver letters?
6. 'Lou Grant' was a spin-off from which American TV series?
7. What was the name of Lady Penelope's butler?
8. With which 60's music programme would you associate Cathy McGowan?
9. Which soap opera is set in Ambridge?
10. Who played the title role in the original TV series of 'Doctor Finlay's Casebook'?
11. Who played the part of the corrupt politician, Michael Murray, in the TV series 'G.B.H.', written by Alan Bleasdale?
12. Which comedian appeared in both the 50's radio series and the late 70's TV version of 'The Glums'?
13. In which fictional town was TV's 'Dad's Army' set?
14. Who was the original host of TV's 'Name That Tune'?
15. In which American TV series would you find the characters Howard, Marion, Richard and Joan Cunningham?
16. What was the name of the first 'Blue Peter' dog?
17. Which quiz programme marked the first appearance of Clive James on television?
18. In which US city is the TV series 'Cheers' based?
19. In which TV series would you have found the characters 'Dave Lister', 'Arnold Rimmer' and 'Cat'?
20. What was the name of Lee Majors' character in the 'Six Million Dollar Man'?
21. Who replaced Patrick Campbell on TV's 'Call My Bluff'?
22. What was the name of the pilot of Fireball XL5?
23. Who starred in the title role of 'Rumpole of the Bailey'?
24. What was the name of the TV chef known as 'The Galloping Gourmet'?

25. Which TV series starring Richard Thomas was based on the book 'Spencer's Mountain'?

26. Which American TV police series starred the characters John Baker and Frank Poncherello?

27. The TV comedy series 'Please, Sir' starring John Alderton, was centred on which school?

28. Who writes and reads 'Letters From America' on the radio?

29. In TV's 'Dr. Who', what do the initials 'TARDIS' stand for?

30. Who played TV's Van der Valk?

31. In which TV comedy series did Barbara Lott play Ronnie Corbett's mother?

32. Who starred alongside Richard Beckinsale in TV's 'The Lovers'?

33. Name the character played by Terence Alexander in 'Bergerac'?

34. On which TV channel does 'Newsnight' appear?

35. What was the name of the carthorse owned by 'Steptoe and Son'?

36. By what name does Robert Robinson refer to Ian Gilles, the question setter on radio's 'Brain of Britain'?

37. Which city hosts the annual 'Golden Rose Awards' ceremony?

38. Which DJ hosted the very first edition of 'Top of the Pops'?

39. Who played the private detective Frank Marker in TV's 'Public Eye'?

40. Which fictional doctor worked at Blair General Hospital?

41. Who created the TV series 'Solo', 'Butterflies' and 'The Mistress'?

42. How was Valentine Dyall better known on the radio?

43. The character Dr. Zachary Smith appeared in which 60's American science fiction series?

44. Who was the original presenter of TV's 'Police Five' in 1962?

45. On whose books was the TV series 'All Creatures Great and Small' based?

46. Which TV programme has been hosted by Noel Edmonds, Jools Holland and David Jacobs?
47. What was the surname of the character played by Leslie Grantham in the soap opera 'Eastenders'?
48. In which TV series did Leonard Rossiter play a character with a cat called Vienna?
49. Which soap opera was originally going to be called 'Florizel Street'?
50. Who was the second actor to play Dr. Who on TV?

Science Quick Questions (*Answers on page 184*)
1.   Where in the human body would you find the Vitreous Humour?
2.   What is the chemical symbol for helium?
3.   Inside which organ is the gall-bladder?
4.   A deficiency of which vitamin causes the disease scurvy?
5.   What colour would litmus paper turn if immersed in an acid?
6.   Which human organ produces insulin?
7.   What is the chemical symbol for tungsten?
8.   Which metal was once called plumbium?
9.   In which country was Albert Einstein born?
10. What name is given to the system of healing developed by Dr. Andrew Still involving the manipulation of the bones of the body?
11. Which boy's name is also the name of the derived S.I. unit of inductance?
12. 'Copper' is named after which island in the Mediterranean?
13. Which gas makes up over 90% of natural gas?
14. Which element has the lowest atomic number?
15. What name is given to the study and use of frequencies beyond the limits of human hearing?
16. In computing terminology, what does the acronym RAM stand for?
17. What is the chemical symbol for gold?
18. What name is given to the lowest layer of the atmosphere?
19. Which planet in the solar system is thought to weigh two and a half times that of all the other planets combined?

20. What type of machine was ENIAC, built in 1946?
21. Name the only surviving mammal of the order *proboscidea*.
22. Which gas takes its name from the Greek for 'saltpetre producer'?
23. Which liquid is used in an aneroid barometer?
24. The name of which synthetic material is taken from parts of the names of two cities?
25. What is polyvinyl chloride more usually called?
26. Which scientist set up the first nuclear reactor in 1942 at the University of Chicago?
27. In physics, the word 'quark' is used to refer to certain basic particles, but which Irish author first coined the term?
28. Which natural element has the highest melting point?
29. According to the Weights and Measures Act 1963, what is the imperial equivalent of 0.9144 metres?
30. Which gas, atomic number 2, is named after the Greek word for 'sun'?
31. Which planet in the solar system takes the longest to spin on its own axis?
32. Which poison is also a metal found in transistors, and an element, atomic number 33?
33. How many acres are there in a square mile?
34. In 1956 Britain opened its first nuclear power station at Calder Hall. In which county was it?
35. Rubies and sapphires are both types of which mineral?
36. Which drug comes from the bark of a cinchona tree?
37. On which planet is the volcano, Olympus Mons?
38. By what name is the discharge of static electricity around the top of tall objects during stormy weather called?
39. What is the common name for the drug acetylsalicylic acid?
40. In geometry, what name is given to a quadrilateral with one pair of sides parallel?
41. Which gas is often referred to as Marsh Gas?
42. What name is given to the male reproductive organ in flowering plants?
43. Which is the predominant gas in the atmosphere of both Venus and Mars?

44. What would be removed in a nephrectomy?
45. Which vitamin is essential for blood clotting?
46. What was the former name of the atomic power station, Sellafield?
47. By what name is the hot and dusty wind that blows from North Africa to Southern Europe, usually in the spring, known?
48. Which metal is added to steel to make it 'stainless steel'?
49. Which anaesthetic was first used in surgery by Sir James Simpson in 1847 and was administered to Queen Victoria at the birth of Prince Leopold in 1853?
50. The discoveries of sodium, magnesium, potassium and calcium are all credited to which scientist?

Sport Quick Questions (*Answers on page 184*)
1. In what kind of swimming race would competitors start in the water rather than by a racing dive?
2. Which country won every Olympic men's hockey gold medal from 1928 to 1964?
3. Which of America's horse-racing Triple Crown is run at Churchill Downs, Louisville?
4. In show-jumping, how many faults are incurred for knocking a fence down?
5. Which game is reputed to have started at Harrow School in the nineteenth century?
6. Which European resort hosted the first Winter Olympic Games in 1924?
7. How many players in a Rugby Union team?
8. Which city hosted the equestrian events for the 1956 Olympic Games?
9. How many feet long is a full-length snooker table?
10. What is the final event in the decathlon?
11. Which swimming stroke was not introduced into the Olympic Games until 1956?
12. In which month is the Epsom Derby now traditionally run?
13. Which sporting event has been successively sponsored by Guinness, Mars and ADT?

14. Which sport may take place in a velodrome?
15. With which sport would you associate the Eisenhower Trophy?
16. Who was the first Frenchman to have been Formula One World Champion?
17. The Isle of Man T.T. Races: what do the letters T.T. stand for?
18. How many players comprise an ice hockey team?
19. Who was the first American to win the Tour de France?
20. In snooker, which colour ball is spotted on the centre of the table?
21. What is the maximum number of gears allowed on a speedway motorcycle?
22. Name *both* English football league clubs for which Stanley Matthews played.
23. In cricket, what do the initials M.C.C. stand for?
24. What is the minimum number of points needed to win a tennis set?
25. Which country usually play their home rugby union matches at Lansdowne Road?
26. Who was Britain's first world heavyweight boxing champion?
27. Which British city hosted the 1970 Commonwealth Games?
28. In horse-racing, what term is given to a horse that has not yet won a race?
29. How many disciplines comprise the men's gymnastic competition at the Olympic Games?
30. Which American swimmer broke seven world records and won seven gold medals at the 1972 Olympic Games?
31. Which of the English horse-racing Classics is run in September?
32. The international governing body of which sport is known as F.I.N.A. – the Fédération Internationale de Natation Amateur?
33. What name is given to the sport which combines cross-country running with map reading?
34. How many riders contest each race in British speedway?

35. Which sport was first devised as a combat sport in 1882 by Dr. Jigoro Kano?

36. Which British golfer won the 1969 British Open?

37. Which batsman scored six sixes in one over for Nottinghamshire in a match against Glamorgan in 1968?

38. Who partnered Owen Davidson to four Wimbledon Mixed Doubles Tennis Championships in the 1960's and 1970's?

39. Which other event combines with cross-country skiing in the Biathlon?

40. Three types of sword are used in fencing. The foil and the épée are two – what is the third?

41. How many rounds make up an amateur boxing match?

42. Which annual championship was first held on 17 October 1860 at Prestwick, Ayrshire, and was won by Willie Park, Sr.?

43. How many greyhounds contest the final of the Greyhound Derby?

44. Which fellow Australian partnered John Newcombe to three successive Wimbledon Men's Doubles titles 1968–70?

45. In Rugby Union, how many matches need to be won to achieve the 'Grand Slam'?

46. Which sport is generally regarded as being the fastest ball game?

47. How many yards are there between each set of stumps in cricket?

48. What name is given to the lightest weight category in Olympic boxing?

49. Name one of the riders who has won the Tour de France on five or more occasions?

50. Which sport was banned in Scotland in 1457?

'Gamble' Questions (*Answers on page 185*)
For the 'Gamble' questions as part of the Social Quiz, not only would I read out the following instructions at the beginning of the session, but if possible, print it on the answer sheet to act as a reminder to the teams.

'At the end of each of the first five rounds I shall be reading out one clue for you to piece together the answer.

If you hand in your paper after hearing only ONE clue – and get it right – your team scores ten points. If you hand it in after hearing two clues, your team scores eight points, and so on.

It is up to you when you hand in your answer paper. However, you only have one chance. If your answer is wrong, you won't score any points for that question at all.'

Question A

Clue 1:   During the First World War, he saw active service in France as commander of the 6th Royal Scots Fusiliers.

Clue 2:   He was the son of a former Chancellor of the Exchequer.

Clue 3:   He included horse-racing, bricklaying and painting among his hobbies.

Clue 4:   He was awarded a Nobel Prize in 1953, the year he was knighted.

Clue 5:   Born in 1874, he had, at various times, been both a Liberal and Conservative Member of Parliament, representing Dundee, Epping, and Oldham.

Question B

Clue 1:   This U.S. state is nicknamed the 'Show Me State' and was at the opposite end of the Pony Express route from California.

Clue 2:   At the end of World War II, the Japanese formally surrendered aboard the U.S. battleship of the same name.

Clue 3:   The nineteenth largest state in terms of area, it is bounded by Iowa to the north and Arkansas to the south.

Clue 4:   The state capital is Jefferson City, although St. Louis is its largest city.

Clue 5:   It is named after the river which is the longest tributary of the Mississippi.

Question C

Clue 1: Born in February 1809, there is a statue of this political leader in Parliament Square in London.

Clue 2: He became a lawyer in 1836 after passing his bar exams.

Clue 3: In 1842 he married Mary Todd, who was officially pronounced insane ten years after his death.

Clue 4: In March 1861 he became the sixteenth President of the United States of America.

Clue 5: He was shot on Good Friday 1865 and died the following morning.

Question D

Clue 1: This comedy actor was born at Ulverston on 16th June 1890, and was educated at King James Grammar School at Bishop Auckland.

Clue 2: He made his stage debut in 1906 in Glasgow, and joined the Fred Karno Company in 1910 just before their tour to the U.S.A.

Clue 3: During this tour he worked as understudy to Charlie Chaplin.

Clue 4: He first appeared in the film 'Nuts in May' in 1917, and made over 70 films in the next nine years.

Clue 5: His and his partner's fan club is called the 'Sons of the Desert' after their 1933 film.

Question E

Clue 1: This writer, the second of eight children, was born on 7th February 1812, the son of a clerk in the Navy pay office.

Clue 2: He edited the memoirs of the famous clown, Joseph Grimaldi.

Clue 3: Buried in Poets' Corner at Westminster Abbey, the centenary of his death was commemorated by a set of five British postage stamps in 1970.

Clue 4: At one stage he reported on House of Commons debates for the Morning Chronicle, and in 1846 he founded the radical newspaper, the Daily News. Many of his earlier works appeared in serialised form.

Clue 5: He died before completing his novel 'The Mystery of Edwin Drood'.

Question F

Clue 1: The son of a clergyman, this man was born in Wiltshire on 20 October 1632.

Clue 2: In 1661 he became Professor of Astronomy at Oxford, and in 1681 he became President of the Royal Society.

Clue 3: He gained an interest in architecture, and his first works were the Sheldonian Theatre at Oxford and the chapel at Pembroke Chapel, Cambridge.

Clue 4: His portrait has appeared on a Bank of England £50 note.

Clue 5: He is buried in St. Paul's Cathedral, where his epitaph is translated as 'If you seek a monument, look about you.'

Question G

Clue 1: This country has an area of over 175,000 square miles, and has a red flag with a green pentagram.

Clue 2: Made up of parts of former French and Spanish protectorates, it is now a hereditary monarchy.

Clue 3: It has both a Mediterranean and an Atlantic coastline.

Clue 4: Its main unit of currency is the dirham, and its capital city is Rabat.

Clue 5: Its biggest city is also the name of a 1942 film starring Humphrey Bogart and Ingrid Bergman.

Question H

Clue 1: This actor first entered show-business as a juggler at Pennsylvania amusement park, and went on to top the bill at the Folies Bergère in Paris and give a command performance at Buckingham Palace in 1901.

Clue 2: From 1906–24 he worked consistently on Broadway and in revues such as the Ziegfeld Follies and, after making many silent movies, his first sound film was 'The Golf Specialist' in 1930.

Clue 3: Also a writer of his own scripts, he used pseudonyms such as Charles Bogle, Mahatma Kane Jeeves and Otis Criblecoblis.

Clue 4: Although noted for his comic roles, his one dramatic role was as Mr. Micawber in 'David Copperfield' in 1935.

Clue 5: His most famous films include 'The Bank Dick' and 'Never Give a Sucker an Even Break'.

Question I

Clue 1: This actor was born in Cleveland, Ohio in 1925, served in the US Navy on torpedo planes as radioman during World War II and gained a degree in economics and dramatics from Kenyon College, Ohio in 1949.

Clue 2: After a spell running the family sporting goods business, he became an actor in 1952 working both on TV and on Broadway before signing a contract with Warner Brothers in 1955.

Clue 3: His first appearance was in the film 'The Silver Chalice', although he later apologized for the film in a celebrated Hollywood trade advertisement.

Clue 4: In 1968 he directed his wife in his first feature film 'Rachel, Rachel'.

Clue 5: He was nominated for a Best Actor Oscar for his performances in 'Cat on a Hot Tin Roof', 'The Hustler', 'Hud' and 'Cool Hand Luke'.

Table Question 1 – Capital Cities (*Answers on page 185*)
The following is a list of countries. All you have to do is to fill in the names of the capital cities for each country. To prevent any arguments the answers are those given in the Whitaker's Almanack.

1.   ALBANIA   ....

2.   ARGENTINA   ....

3.   AUSTRALIA   ....

4.   BRAZIL   ....

5.   BULGARIA   ....

6.   CANADA   ....

7.   CHILE   ....

8.   DENMARK   ....

9.   GHANA   ....

10.   GREECE   ....

11.   IRAN   ....

12.   IRAQ   ....

13.   KENYA   ....

14.   LAOS   ....

15.   LIBYA   ....

16.   LIECHTENSTEIN   ....

17.   MOROCCO   ....

18.   NEW ZEALAND   ....

19.   NEPAL   ....

20.   NIGERIA   ....

21.   PANAMA   ....

22.   SAUDI ARABIA   ....

23. SWITZERLAND   ....

24. TURKEY   ....

25. VIETNAM   ....

Table Question 2 – Years (*Answers on page 185*)
The following groups of events each happened in a different year, from 1960 to 1979. All you have to do is to write in the correct year next to each group!

A. .... Yuri Gagarin becomes first man in space.
                     Berlin Wall erected.
                     Tottenham Hotspur win 'the double'.
B. .... Geoff Hurst scores a hat-trick at Wembley.
                     Plaid Cymru win by-election at Carmarthen.
                     Commonwealth Games held at Kingston, Jamaica.
C. .... 'Je T'Aime Moi Non Plus' banned by BBC.
                     Apollo 11 lands two astronauts on the moon.
                     First colour programmes on British TV.
D. .... Taiwan expelled from U.N. Security Council.
                     Mill Reef wins the English Derby.
                     Rod Stewart tops UK hit parade with 'Maggie May'.
E. .... Lord Mountbatten killed by bomb explosion.
                     Ayatollah Khomeini returns to Iran from exile.
                     First visit of Pope to Ireland.
F. .... Start of Freddie Laker's Skytrain service to the USA.
                     Death of Charlie Chaplin.
                     Birth of first grandchild of Queen Elizabeth II.
G. .... Resignation of John Profumo M.P.
                     Great Train Robbery.
                     Assassination of John F. Kennedy.
H. .... Release of 'The Sting' starring Redford and Newman.
                     Britain joins E.E.C.

Red Rum wins the Grand National for the first time.

I. .... Cuban missile crisis.

The Beatles have their first chart success.

Launch of Telstar.

J. .... President Nixon resigns.

Muhammad Ali regains World Heavyweight Boxing Championship.

British General Election produces no overall majority.

K. .... Birth of first 'test tube' baby.

Three Popes in one year.

Several hundred religious cultists die in mass suicide in Guyana.

L. .... Sandie Shaw's 'Puppet on a String' wins Eurovision Song Contest.

Deaths of Donald Campbell and Che Guevara.

Arab/Israeli 'Six Day War'.

M. .... Harold Wilson becomes Prime Minister.

Jean Paul Sartre declines Nobel Prize.

Nelson Mandela sentenced to life imprisonment.

N. .... Conservative Party win general election.

Deaths of de Gaulle and Nasser.

Chelsea win F.A. Cup after a replay.

O. .... 'Bloody Sunday' in Northern Ireland.

Bangladesh joins the Commonwealth.

Bobby Fischer becomes World Chess Champion.

P. .... Margaret Thatcher becomes Conservative Party Leader.

Death of General Franco.

Vietcong enter Saigon.

Q. .... Rhodesia declares U.D.I.

Death of Sir Winston Churchill.

Release of the film 'The Sound of Music'.

R. .... Assassinations of Martin Luther King and Robert Kennedy.

Introduction of two-tier postage system.
Russian troops invade Czechoslovakia.
S. .... James Callaghan becomes Prime Minister.
Bjorn Borg wins Wimbledon's singles title for
the first time.
Israeli commandos free hostages at Entebbe.
T. .... Sharpeville massacre in South Africa.
Wolverhampton Wanderers win F.A. Cup.
U2 spy plane shot down over USSR.

Table Question 3 – Countries (*Answers on page 186*)
The following is a list of countries who have now changed their
names. We list their old names . . . all you have to do is list
their current names.

1.   ....Gold Coast

2.   ....Abyssinia

3.   ....Ceylon

4.   ....British Honduras

5.   ....Northern Rhodesia

6.   ....Aden

7.   ....British Guiana

8.   ....Belgian Congo

9.   ....Upper Volta

10.   ....Hejaz-Nejd

11.   ....Persia

12.   ....East Pakistan

13.   ....Nyasaland

14.   ....French Somaliland

15.   ....Portuguese Guinea

16.   ....French Sudan

17.   ....Rhodesia

18.   ....Dutch Guinea

19.   ....Siam

20.   ....Dutch East Indies

Table Question 4 – Film Anagrams (*Answers on page 186*)
The following is a list of famous film titles, carefully jumbled to
make it more difficult for you to identify them. All you have to
do is to solve the anagrams and name the films.

1.   ....CHOPSY

2.   ....LONG FRIDGE

3.   ....DAN THE MIRTH

4.   ....BRING HOT CORK

5.   ....NOW I WED THE THING

6.   ....THESE FLAT COALMEN

7.   ....RIGHT DATE TO TRACE

8.   ....CONE IN FUR BERET

9.   ....POOR COB

10.   ....GET PEACHES RATE

11.   ....AND CASH WILL FADE A

12.   ....THE DEATH FROG

13.   ....OF AUTOCAR IF

14.   ....ROYAL KEG

15.   ....IN THE EVENT CAME FINGS

16.   ....MUST ROCK ON

17.   ....O BLAST CORNY CRANE

18.   ....A STOP IN A STARLING

19.   ....NO TO PAL

20.   ....HEART OF CAP

Table Question 5 – Which County? (*Answers on page 186*)
Each of the following lists a number of places that are all found
in the same English county. All you have to do is to give the
name of the relevant county next to the appropriate number.

1.   Corfe Castle, Milton Abbey and the Cerne Giant?
2.   Flatford Mill, Gainsborough's House and Framlingham
      Castle?
3.   Wells Cathedral and the site of the Battle of Sedgemoor?
4.   Oakham Castle, Ashby-de-la-Zouch Castle, Grace Road
      Cricket Ground and the site of the Battle of Bosworth?
5.   Tatton Hall, Gawsworth Hall and Jodrell Bank?
6.   Longleat, Stonehenge and Avebury?
7.   Alton Towers, Cannock Chase and Lichfield Cathedral?
8.   Brands Hatch, Leeds Castle and Walmer Castle?
9.   Beaulieu Motor Museum, HMS Victory and the birth-

place of Jane Austen?
10. Pilkington Glass Museum, Walker Art Gallery and Haydock Park Racecourse?
11. Woburn Abbey, Kenilworth Road Football Ground and Whipsnade Zoo?
12. Bodleian Library, Blenheim Palace and the Iffley Road Running Track (where Bannister first broke the four-minute mile)?
13. Earls Barton Church, Fotheringay Castle and the Watford Gap Service Station?
14. Ormesby Hall, Guisborough Priory, Captain James Cook Museum and Redcar Racecourse?
15. The oldest service station on the M25?
16. Eton College, Sandhurst and Greenham Common?
17. Imperial War Museum, Fitzwilliam Museum, Cromwell Museum and Grafham Water?
18. The only county having land borders with only one other English county?
19. Anne Hathaway's Cottage, Kenilworth Castle and most of the Forest of Arden?
20. Chatsworth House, Repton School and the Baseball Ground?

Table Question 6 – Olympic Venues (*Answers on page 186*)
Name the host cities of the Summer Olympic Games in each of the following years.

1. 1948
2. 1952
3. 1956
4. 1960
5. 1964
6. 1968
7. 1972
8. 1976
9. 1980
10. 1984
11. 1988
12. 1992

Table Question 7 – Sports (*Answers on page 187*)
In which sport have the following been World or Olympic
Champions?

1.   David Bryant   ....

2.   Hans Nielsen   ....

3.   Martine Le Moignan   ....

4.   Malcolm Cooper   ....

5.   Richard Bergmann   ....

6.   Darrell Pace   ....

7.   Yang Yang   ....

8.   Vladimir Salnikov   ....

9.   Eddie Lawson   ....

10. Naoya Ogawa   ....

11. Scott Hamilton   ....

12. Phil Taylor   ....

13. Boris Onischenko   ....

14. Phil Hill   ....

15. John Spencer   ....

16. Hugh Porter   ....

17. Nelli Kim   ....

18. Greg Louganis   ....

19. Mark Wildman   ....

20. Mike Hazelwood   ....

Table Question 8 – Pop Music (*Answers on page 187*)
Name the artists who were the first to have a UK number one
hit single with the following songs:

1.   When The Going Gets Tough, The Tough Get Going
2.   Smoke Gets In Your Eyes
3.   Mamma Mia
4.   Secret Love
5.   Tell Laura I Love Her
6.   19
7.   Ring My Bell
8.   Unchained Melody
9.   Stand and Deliver
10. Clair
11. With A Girl Like You
12. Shaddap You Face
13. Dance On
14. The Lion Sleeps Tonight
15. Puppy Love
16. Woodstock
17. Video Killed The Radio Star
18. The Sun Always Shines on TV
19. Call Me
20. She
21. Only You
22. I Pretend
23. Silver Lady
24. Billy Don't Be A Hero
25. West End Girls

Table Question 9 – 'Call My Bluff' (*Answers on page 187*)
Indicate which of the three alternatives best explains each of the
words on the left.

A. ALIFORM
- a) identical
- b) wing-shaped
- c) having feathers

B. BARYON
- a) the tip of a tree root
- b) a chemical element
- c) an elementary particle

C. CATCHPOLE
- a) a medieval officer who arrested debtors
- b) a Scottish election agent
- c) a large stick used to vault canals

D. DIGAMY
- a) a second marriage
- b) a two-wheeled chariot
- c) an archaeological excavation

E. EUPHOTIC
- a) pleasant to hear
- b) a drug which induces elation
- c) the uppermost part of a sea or lake

F. FRIABLE
- a) edible
- b) crumbly
- c) capable of being pronounced

G. GUCK
- a) slimy matter
- b) to bend or to change direction
- c) a fish dish containing olives

H. HOGGIN
- a) a young male pig
- b) a medieval cask
- c) finely sifted gravel

I. **ICHNITE**
a) a fossilized footprint
b) a member of a Celtic religious sect
c) an element found in meteorites

J. **JUKSKEI**
a) a Russian gypsy
b) a Yugoslavian dance
c) a South African game

K. **KOKAKO**
a) a Japanese woodwind instrument
b) a New Zealand wattled crow
c) a Hawaiian parrot

L. **LINCRUSTA**
a) a type of wallpaper
b) a type of scorpion
c) painted lines on grass

M. **MIDIRON**
a) the board used in mah-jong
b) scrap left after smelting
c) a No. 2 iron used in golf

N. **NIPA**
a) a jumping flea
b) a South American fruit
c) a pine tree

O. **OROGENY**
a) the formation of mountain ranges
b) the study of sensitivity
c) the Chinese art of fortune-telling

P. **POMELO**
a) a whimsical poem or ode
b) a saddle used on donkeys
c) a citrus fruit

Q. **QINDAR**
a) an African pygmy deer
b) an Albanian unit of currency
c) a radioactive particle

R. RESTHARROW
a) a plant with woody stems and roots
b) a German roadside inn
c) a breed of dogs used for hunting foxes

S. SCOW
a) a freight-barge
b) an oatmeal cake
c) a thick shawl

T. TEOCALLI
a) a truncated Aztec pyramid
b) a style of Renaissance architecture
c) star-shaped pasta

U. URSINE
a) pig-like
b) bear-like
c) hairy

V. VIGORO
a) any fast growing grass such as bamboo
b) an Australian women's game like cricket
c) a musical term denoting extremely fast

W. WITHERSHINS
a) antisocial
b) anticlockwise
c) antimagnetic

X. XEROSIS
a) a psychological disorder
b) the duplication of items
c) abnormal dryness of bodily tissues

Y. YULAN
a) a Chinese magnolia
b) a Mexican wine
c) an Islamic festival

Z. ZANDER
a) a bird
b) a fish
c) a salamander

6

ANSWERS

General Knowledge 1 – Answers
1. On an English £1 coin
2. £350
3. University Boat Race
4. Ireland
5. Statue of Liberty
6. Colorado *or* Wyoming
7. Q
8. Epsilon
9. Teddy Bears
10. Zephaniah

General Knowledge 2 – Answers
1. Stamford Bridge
2. Government Chief Whip
3. 225
4. El Cid
5. Red, white and blue
6. Angostura bitters
7. D
8. 21
9. Cornwall
10. P (they are the first letters of the planets in order from the sun: P is for Pluto)

General Knowedge 3 – Answers
1. Esperanto
2. 4
3. Postcards
4. Capricorn
5. Tunisia
6. Red
7. Daihatsu
8. 5
9. 28
10. Silver (they all relate to anniversaries)

General Knowledge 4 – Answers
1. Spain
2. Earache
3. Sherlock Holmes
4. Whooping Cough
5. Both have been married to Denis Thatcher
6. 20
7. Television
8. Matchbox Labels
9. Duke of Windsor
10. Champagne

General Knowledge 5 – Answers
1. Flags
2. Four
3. Fishplates
4. Elizabeth II
5. Birmingham

6. Finland
7. 42 years
8. Sunday Express
9. York
10. Old Kent Road

General Knowledge 6 – Answers
1. John F. Kennedy
2. John Maynard Keynes
3. Brown
4. Brown
5. Elizabeth Garrett Anderson
6. Malachi
7. Edwin ('Buzz') Aldrin
8. General George Patton
9. Halifax
10. M – (letters on the bottom line of a typewriter keyboard)

General Knowledge 7 – Answers
1. One million
2. The Boys Brigade
3. G
4. Twelve
5. Bell-ringing
6. Orange
7. Fifteen
8. Jeremy Thorpe
9. Economics
10. La Paz

General Knowledge 8 – Answers
1. 5%
2. The big toe
3. David Elsworth
4. The English Channel
5. Race
6. Ten
7. On Mount Sinai (which is in the south of the Sinai peninsula)
8. All are American state capitals
9. For Gallantry
10. 1900 only

General Knowledge 9 – Answers
1. Twenty years
2. Mount Rushmore
3. Royal Hospital, Chelsea
4. A links course is by the sea
5. Kentucky
6. Neville Chamberlain
7. Blue
8. Chicken Marengo
9. Dag Hammarskjold
10. Marquesses

General Knowledge 10 – Answers
1. Northern Line
2. Seven
3. Red *and* amber (traffic light sequence)
4. Libra
5. Entrechat
6. Green *and* yellow
7. The Boys Brigade
8. Coleraine
9. 40
10. 1,666 (the numerals being MDCLXVI)

General Knowledge 11 – Answers
1. River Dee
2. Norwegian (Trygve Lie)
3. Astronauts
4. Isle of Wight
5. Green
6. Iceland
7. Entertainments National Service Association
8. St. Augustine

9.   Daily Express
10. Anthony Trollope

General Knowledge 12 – Answers
1.   Luxembourg
2.   George Fox
3.   York
4.   The losers' ribbons
5.   Harvard
6.   Yellow
7.   Black Monday, a stock market crash
8.   Yom Kippur (Day of Atonement)
9.   Memphis
10. V.J. Day

General Knowledge 13 – Answers
1.   Marie Curie
2.   France
3.   The Moon
4.   Crystal Palace
5.   Air Marshal
6.   Hinduism
7.   Amelia Earhart
8.   Jesse James
9.   H.M.S. Beagle
10. Chess

General Knowledge 14 – Answers
1.   The ten shilling note
2.   3
3.   Civil Service
4.   American Express
5.   The hovercraft
6.   Sir Henry Irving
7.   None
8.   Liver
9.   Lloyds
10. Parliament

General Knowledge 15 – Answers
1.   Evening Star
2.   Daily Mail
3.   African Violet
4.   Swan
5.   Iraq
6.   The White House
7.   Seven
8.   Bill Shankly
9.   1010
10. Map of the London Underground

General Knowledge 16 – Answers
1.   10 (clockwise sequence of numbers on a dartboard)
2.   Motorcycle
3.   'I'
4.   Old Vic
5.   Renault
6.   Sir Bedevere
7.   David Low
8.   35 years
9.   Washington D.C.
10. Melbourne

General Knowledge 17 – Answers
1.   Seven
2.   Czech
3.   Sense of smell
4.   One
5.   Twelve
6.   Jupiter
7.   8
8.   154 square inches
9.   17 (11 in the fielding side, two umpires, two batsmen and their two runners)
10. 26

General Knowledge 18 – Answers

1. Change from the Julian to the Gregorian calendar
2. Standard railway gauge
3. M.P.s (or parliamentary constituencies)
4. Join the League of Nations
5. Margaret (*real* first names of British Prime Ministers)
6. Their flags are red, white and blue
7. Landlocked (they have no coastline)
8. Edinburgh
9. All winners of the English Derby
10. Silver content of 'silver' coins

Acronyms – Answers

1. Organisation of Petroleum Exporting Countries
2. People's Dispensary for Sick Animals
3. Southeast Asia Treaty Organisation
4. Strategic Arms Limitation Talks (or Treaty)
5. Navy, Army and Air Force Institutes
6. Electronic Random Number Indicator Equipment
7. Advisory Conciliation and Arbitration Service
8. United Nations Educational, Scientific and Cultural Organisation
9. Self-contained Underwater Breathing Apparatus
10. Market and Opinion Research Institute

Aliases 1 – Answers

1. Big Daddy
2. George Eliot
3. Cary Grant
4. Boris Karloff
5. Boy George
6. Michael Caine
7. Elton John
8. Trotsky
9. Fred Astaire
10. Marilyn Monroe

Aliases 2 – Answers

1. Judy Garland
2. Cher
3. Greta Garbo
4. Dame Anna Neagle
5. Bob Dylan
6. Twiggy
7. Sting
8. Cliff Richard
9. Englebert Humperdinck
10. Pele

Aliases 3 – Answers

1. John Wayne
2. Laurence Harvey
3. Lewis Carroll
4. Lord Haw-Haw
5. David Bowie
6. Woody Allen
7. George Orwell
8. Mata Hari
9. John Le Carré
10. El Greco

Art 1 – Answers

1. St. Petersburg
2. The Clore Gallery
3. Pre-Raphaelite Brotherhood

4. Fresco
5. Michelangelo
6. Madrid
7. Crete
8. Paul Gauguin
9. A Rake's Progress
10. The British Museum

Art 2 – Answers
1. Florence
2. Michelangelo
3. Triptych
4. Brown
5. Graham Sutherland
6. David Hockney
7. Andy Warhol
8. Victoria and Albert Museum
9. Claude Monet
10. George Stubbs

Assassinations – Answers
1. Sarajevo
2. New York
3. Jean Paul Marat
4. Casca
5. Hendrick Verwoerd
6. 1968
7. Indira Ghandi
8. William McKinley
9. Washington
10. Mexico (he was better known as Trotsky)

The Bible – Answers
1. Eight
2. Deuteronomy
3. Obadiah
4. Andrew
5. David
6. Sixth day

7. Paul's Epistle to the Romans
8. Seth
9. Philistine
10. Pentateuch

Birds 1 – Answers
1. Puck
2. Eagle ('The Eagle Has Landed')
3. One
4. Cuckoo
5. Saxophone
6. Daphne Du Maurier
7. Albatross
8. Norwegian Blue
9. Crystal Palace
10. Barclays

Birds 2 – Answers
1. Ducks
2. Dunnock
3. Ostrich
4. Murder
5. Ravens
6. Cuckoo
7. Hummingbird
8. New Zealand
9. Wren
10. Australia

Books and Films – Answers
1. Beau Geste
2. The Four Feathers
3. The Wizard of Oz
4. Alistair MacLean
5. One Flew Over the Cuckoo's Nest
6. Mary Poppins
7. 2001: A Space Odyssey
8. Gone With The Wind

9. Stephen King
10. Ian Fleming

City And Finance – Answers
1. Unlisted Securities Market
2. Share price levels on the Hong Kong Stock Exchange
3. A stag
4. Threadneedle Street
5. Chief Cashier of the Bank of England (their signatures have all appeared on banknotes)
6. Mortgage Interest Relief at Source
7. The South Sea Bubble
8. 30
9. Milan
10. Personal Equity Plan

Coins and Medals – Answers
1. 63
2. Two pence
3. 12
4. Wren
5. For Valour
6. Equal
7. Death of Sir Winston Churchill
8. Indian Independence
9. Congressional Medal of Honour
10. Printing

Currencies – Answers
1. Markka
2. Dollar
3. Shilling
4. Rupee
5. Dinar
6. Dollar

7. Riyal
8. Dirham
9. Peso
10. Yuan (or Renminbi)

Famous Animals – Answers
1. Scout
2. Pickles
3. Toto
4. Cheetah
5. Pandas
6. Nipper
7. Richard Adams
8. Dog
9. Bull's Eye
10. Bear

Films 1 – Answers
1. Empire of the Sun
2. The Elephant Man
3. The Birdman of Alcatraz
4. Van Gogh
5. Scandal
6. Gladys Aylward
7. Paris
8. Robert Redford *and* Dustin Hoffman
9. James Stewart
10. Spike Milligan

Films 2 – Answers
1. The Misfits
2. The Slipper and the Rose
3. Peter O'Toole
4. Salvador Dali
5. National Velvet
6. Patton – Lust for Glory
7. Carry On Sergeant
8. Paramount
9. Dr. Zhivago
10. Australia

Films 3 – Answers
1. The Robe
2. Gorky Park
3. Vietnam War
4. Snow White and the Seven Dwarfs
5. Robin Hood
6. Sherlock Holmes
7. Paul Newman
8. Ben Kingsley
9. W.C. Fields
10. Fort Apache

Films 4 – Blue Movies – Answers
1. Marlene Dietrich
2. Alistair Sim
3. Angela Lansbury
4. World War I
5. Jean Simmons
6. Buffy St. Marie
7. Biloxi Blues
8. Helicopters
9. Dan Aykroyd
10. Dirk Bogarde

Film Directors – Answers
1. Sergei Eisenstein
2. David Lean
3. Carol Reed
4. Michael Curtiz
5. Francis Ford Coppola
6. Michael Cimino
7. Leonard Nimoy
8. Mel Brooks
9. Nick Roeg
10. Paul Newman

Film Sequels – Answers
1. The Invisible Man
2. Star Trek II: The Wrath of Khan
3. Tom Cruise
4. The Godfather Part II
5. Stardust
6. Love Story
7. Alan Price
8. The Four Musketeers
9. Psycho
10. Rooster Cogburn

Film Title Roles 1 – Answers
1. Peter O'Toole
2. Michael Keaton
3. Joseph Wiseman
4. Robert Redford
5. Charlie Chaplin
6. Al Pacino
7. David Bowie
8. Kenneth More
9. Jane Fonda
10. Frank Morgan

Film Title Roles 2 – Answers
1. Frank Sinatra
2. Michael Caine
3. Elizabeth Taylor
4. Jacques Tati
5. Dirk Bogarde
6. Bela Lugosi
7. Errol Flynn
8. John Hurt
9. Vanessa Redgrave
10. Ursula Andress

Firsts – Answers
1. Matterhorn
2. Uruguay
3. First woman in space
4. A heart transplant
5. Oxford
6. Delaware
7. Elvis Presley

8. Letchworth
9. Robert Peary
10. Postage stamps

Food and Drink 1 – Answers
1. Prunes *and* bacon
2. Pavlova
3. Gin
4. Bath
5. Spinach
6. Portugal
7. Tomato
8. Nine
9. Beetroot
10. Mexico

Food and Drink 2 – Answers
1. Cabbage
2. Courgette
3. Belgium
4. Brandy
5. Grapes
6. Newton and Ridley
7. Two
8. Pina Colada
9. Very Special (or Superior) Old Pale
10. Gas Mark 2

Food and Drink 3 – Answers
1. Tequila
2. Norwich
3. Saffron
4. Nectarine
5. Herrings
6. 7
7. Buffalo
8. Gold
9. Choux pastry
10. A Nebuchadnezzar (sizes of wine bottles)

Football – Answers
1. Di Stefano
2. Ian Rush
3. Kenny Dalglish
4. London
5. Bobby Moore
6. Pele
7. Glasgow Rangers
8. Wolverhampton Wanderers
9. Billy Wright
10. Stanley Matthews

Geography 1 – Answers
1. The Philippines
2. Jersey
3. Abu Dhabi
4. Mali
5. Asuncion
6. Liechtenstein
7. Basle
8. Lake Michigan
9. Brussels
10. Cuba

Geography 2 – Answers
1. Europe
2. River Tagus
3. Sahara Desert
4. Andorra
5. Oslo
6. Korea
7. Hindi
8. Indian Ocean
9. Uganda
10. Alaska

Geography 3 – Answers
1. Austin
2. Corsica
3. Romania
4. Bass Strait

5.   Lake Michigan
6.   River Tay
7.   Isobar
8.   Atlantic Ocean
9.   Orkney Islands
10. Caspian Sea

Geography 4 – Answers
1.   Isohyet
2.   Orkneys
3.   Canada
4.   Cairo
5.   Scilly Isles
6.   Anglesey
7.   Suffolk
8.   Australia
9.   Andes
10. Preston

Geography 5 – Answers
1.   Australia
2.   India
3.   Canada
4.   Catalan
5.   Hawaii
6.   Youth Hostel
7.   Canada
8.   India
9.   Canary Islands
10. Wellington

Geography 6 – Answers
1.   Germany
2.   Gloucestershire
3.   Aden
4.   Hoover Dam
5.   Berne
6.   Peak District
7.   Chile
8.   Rio De Janeiro
9.   South Australia

10. Mongolia

History 1 – Answers
1.   Winston Churchill
2.   He assassinated the British Prime Minister (Spencer Perceval)
3.   Lord Salisbury
4.   Alexander the Great
5.   Spain
6.   Anne Boleyn
7.   Captain of the Titanic
8.   The River Thames
9.   Torrey Canyon
10. Benito Mussolini

History 2 – Answers
1.   Pitt the Elder (Earl of Chatham)
2.   Operation Barbarossa
3.   Edward VI
4.   Stanley Baldwin
5.   Tudor
6.   Friedrich Engels
7.   Grandson
8.   France
9.   Hugh Gaitskell
10. Chile

History 3 – Answers
1.   Richard III (at Bosworth Field)
2.   Winchester
3.   Henry VII
4.   Brother
5.   Dwight D. Eisenhower
6.   Stanley Baldwin
7.   Finland
8.   Idi Amin
9.   Genghis Khan
10. By throwing herself under

the King's horse in the
Derby

History 4 – Answers
1. Eton
2. Dr. Hawley Crippen
3. Wittenburg
4. Charles I
5. Denmark
6. Newcastle
7. Robert E. Lee
8. Somerville College
9. Louis XIV
10. Aristotle

History 5 – Answers
1. St. Alban
2. Aneurin Bevan
3. Edward VIII (the Duke of
   Windsor)
4. Prince Rupert
5. Isambard Kingdom Brunel
6. Brazil
7. Hannibal
8. Francis I
9. Constantine
10. Leningrad

History 6 – Answers
1. Catherine of Aragon
2. St. Helena
3. Whitehall Palace
4. Ermine Street
5. George III
6. He crowned himself
7. York
8. Sir John Vanbrugh
9. Konrad Adenauer
10. Sicily

Husbands and Wives – Answers
1. Nicky Hilton

2. Lady Godiva
3. MacMillan
4. David McCallum
5. Helen of Troy
6. George V
7. John Alderton
8. Ted Hughes
9. Betty
10. Carrie Fisher

Indoor Games – Answers
1. 8
2. Canasta
3. 5
4. 9
5. 168
6. 26
7. 24
8. 1 club
9. Kings Cross
10. Chess

International Organisations – Answers
1. Addis Ababa
2. New York
3. World Meteorological
   Organisation
4. European Community
   (originally the EEC)
5. Red Crescent
6. Yugoslavia
7. Five
8. Luxembourg
9. EFTA (European Free
   Trade Association)
10. Amnesty International

Literary Characters – Answers
1. Bram Stoker
2. Baroness Orczy

3. Agatha Christie
4. Mickey Spillane
5. Beatrix Potter
6. Frank Richards
7. J.R.R. Tolkien
8. Len Deighton
9. Arthur C. Clarke
10. Charles Dickens

Literature 1 – Answers
1. Two Gentlemen of Verona
2. John Donne
3. Gogol
4. Grossmith
5. David Copperfield
6. Brutus
7. Lord Peter Wimsey
8. Rudyard Kipling
9. Cecil Day-Lewis
10. P.G. Wodehouse

Literature 2 – Answers
1. Lady Chatterley's Lover
2. 20 years
3. Agatha Christie
4. Somerset Maugham
5. Casino Royale
6. 25th January
7. Mrs. Malaprop
8. Dashiell Hammett
9. Montmorency
10. Seven (Henry IV Parts 1 and 2, Henry V, Henry VI Parts 1, 2 and 3, and Henry VIII)

Literature 3 (Animals) – Answers
1. Don Quixote
2. Anna Sewell
3. A pig
4. White

5. Horse
6. Aslan
7. Sapper
8. Flamingoes
9. Snake
10. The Taming of the Shrew

Literature 4 (Authors) – Answers
1. Harold Robbins
2. T.S. Eliot
3. Kurt Vonnegut Jr.
4. Aldous Huxley
5. Joseph Heller
6. George Orwell
7. Sir Arthur Conan Doyle
8. Daniel Defoe
9. Roald Dahl
10. Margaret Mitchell

Literature 5 (Shakespeare) – Answers
1. Billiards
2. The Merry Wives of Windsor
3. Twelfth Night or What You Will
4. Hamlet
5. Julius Caesar
6. Malcolm
7. A bear
8. Romeo and Juliet
9. Two Gentlemen of Verona
10. A Midsummer Night's Dream

Middle Names – Answers
1. Sebastian Coe
2. T.S. Eliot
3. He did not have one (the 'S' was just for effect!)
4. Sir William Gilbert

5. Prince Henry
6. J.R.R. Tolkien
7. Paul (his real name is James Paul McCartney)
8. Dylan
9. Oscar Wilde
10. Daley Thompson

Missing Links 1 – Answers
1. Breeds of sheep
2. Typefaces
3. Potatoes
4. Scrooge
5. Apple
6. Nobel Prize Winners (for Literature)
7. 'My Way'
8. Seaweed
9. Marathon
10. Currencies

Missing Links 2 – Answers
1. Suits in a Tarot pack
2. Chancellor of the Exchequer
3. Pigs
4. British Patron Saints' days
5. Defences used in chess openings
6. Chinese years
7. Codenames of D-Day landing beaches
8. Sausages
9. Napkin folds
10. Ducks

Missing Links 3 – Answers
1. 'The Tempest'
2. Butterflies
3. Tea
4. Bricks

5. Paper
6. Months in the Jewish calendar
7. Cheese
8. The Pickwick Club
9. Jonathan King
10. Lighthouses

Missing Links 4 – Answers
1. Yoga
2. Time-zones in the USA
3. Franz Haydn
4. Roses
5. Pasta
6. Nails
7. St. Leger
8. Cattle
9. Motorway service stations
10. 'White Christmas'

Music 1 – Answers
1. Paul Simon
2. Duke Ellington
3. It Doesn't Matter Any More
4. Sir Charles Halle
5. Duran Duran
6. Finnish
7. Rule Britannia
8. Sir Thomas Beecham
9. Waterloo
10. Yesterday

Music 2 – Answers
1. Philip Sousa
2. Living Doll
3. Wendy Richard
4. Bing Crosby
5. 47
6. Bob Dylan
7. It's All Over Now
8. Irving Berlin

9.   Sixth
10. You'll Never Walk Alone

Music 3 – Answers
1.   Madonna
2.   The Unfinished Symphony
3.   Double Bass
4.   Queen
5.   Siouxsie and the Banshees
6.   Piccolo
7.   Jeremiah Clarke
8.   Hector Berlioz
9.   Leonard Bernstein
10. All You Need Is Love

Music 4 – Answers
1.   All Shook Up
2.   Borodin
3.   Glenn Miller
4.   Lento
5.   Rod Stewart
6.   Simon and Garfunkel
7.   Flowers In The Rain
8.   Prokofiev
9.   Venus
10. From Me To You

Music 5 – Answers
1.   Kiki Dee
2.   Pizzicato
3.   Trumpet
4.   Abba
5.   Leon
6.   Rossini
7.   Cliff Richard
8.   Iolanthe
9.   Stravinsky
10. 500,000

Music 6 – Answers
1.   16

2.   Bizet
3.   Matt Monro
4.   Liszt
5.   Prince
6.   Nine
7.   Carmen
8.   India
9.   Tamla Motown
10. T'Pau

Music 7 – Answers
1.   Kate Bush
2.   Ivor Novello
3.   Sandie Shaw
4.   Aaron Copland
5.   Neil Diamond
6.   Rivers of Babylon
7.   Our Man in Havana
8.   The Stranglers
9.   Burt Bacharach
10. Any three from . . .
     Eleanor Rigby, Lady
     Madonna, Hey Jude, The
     Ballad of John and Yoko
     and Penny Lane!

Music and Films – Answers
1.   Zither
2.   John Williams
3.   Shirley Bassey
4.   Blackboard Jungle
5.   Elton John
6.   Clint Eastwood
7.   Rocky III
8.   Love Me Tender
9.   Wilfrid Brambell
10. Tchaikovsky

Mythology 1 – Answers
1.   Mars
2.   Thor

3. Gorgons
4. Cassandra
5. Cerberus
6. Jackal
7. Cyclops
8. Charon
9. Hermes
10. Dido

Mythology 2 – Answers
1. The owl
2. King Arthur
3. Apollo
4. Ireland
5. Pigs
6. Daedalus
7. Grendel
8. Janus
9. Phrygia
10. Poseidon

Mythology 3 – Answers
1. Ambrosia
2. Perseus
3. Priam
4. Theseus
5. Ra (*or* Re)
6. Cortes
7. Pegasus
8. Prometheus
9. Boar
10. Saturn

Natural History – Answers
1. Birds
2. Topiary
3. Magpie
4. Chile
5. Pansy
6. Fish
7. Kangaroos
8. Conchologist
9. Busy Lizzie
10. Claws

Newspapers – Answers
1. Pink
2. Washington Post
3. Times
4. Daily Worker
5. Italy
6. The Observer
7. The Los Angeles Tribune
8. Daily Telegraph
9. Daily Mirror
10. The Mail On Sunday

Numbers – Answers
1. 51
2. 18
3. 99
4. 55
5. 78
6. 4077
7. 4
8. 9
9. 30
10. 1,165

Parliament – Answers
1. Lord Chancellor
2. Thomas Hansard
3. Queen Anne
4. Red
5. 40
6. Lord Chancellor
7. Robert Walpole
8. Tony Benn
9. Herbert Asquith
10. Sir Thomas More

Quotations – Answers
1. Mark Twain

2.   Thomas Edison
3.   Groucho Marx
4.   Mae West
5.   John F. Kennedy
6.   Dr. Johnson
7.   Sir Winston Churchill
8.   Queen Mary I
9.   Julius Caesar
10. Richard Nixon

Radio and Television 1 – Answers
1.   It's That Man Again
2.   Crossroads
3.   Department of
     Administrative Affairs
4.   Sooty
5.   Gary Burghoff
6.   Rock Follies
7.   Eight
8.   Norman Stanley Fletcher
9.   Gerald Seymour
10. Peter Bowles

Radio and Television 2 – Answers
1.   Bedrock
2.   Three
3.   Batman and Robin
4.   Tommy Cooper
5.   Ringo Starr
6.   Piccadilly
7.   Number 6
8.   Denver
9.   Mastermind
10. Thank Your Lucky Stars

Radio and Television 3 – Answers
1.   Cavendish Foods
2.   Max Bygraves
3.   Tony Blackburn
4.   Dangerman
5.   Lewis

6.   Julian Pettifer
7.   Postman Pat
8.   Steve McQueen
9.   Tiberius
10. The Girl From UNCLE

Rivers – Answers
1.   Cam
2.   Trent
3.   Derwent
4.   Taff
5.   Ribble
6.   Witham
7.   Ouse
8.   Yeo
9.   Dee
10. Stour

Science 1 – Answers
1.   Sulphuric acid
2.   Steel
3.   Copper *and* zinc
4.   Uranus
5.   Potassium
6.   −40 (Fahrenheit)
7.   Diamonds
8.   Platinum
9.   Knee-cap
10. 9

Science 2 – Answers
1.   Sir Isaac Newton
2.   Fungi
3.   Chickenpox
4.   Amplitude modulation
5.   Fish
6.   Sn
7.   Fireworks
8.   80
9.   Mercury
10. Marie Curie

Science 3 – Answers
1. Cape Town
2. Sulphuric acid
3. Gums
4. Vitamin C
5. Epsom Salts
6. Nitrogen
7. Read only memory
8. Four
9. Earth
10. Aurora Australis

Science 4 – Answers
1. Polish
2. Proton
3. Platinum
4. Jupiter
5. Isosceles triangle
6. Nose-bleeding
7. Hydrogen
8. Boyle's Law
9. A calorie
10. Wilhelm Röntgen

Sport 1 – Answers
1. Caroline Bradley
2. Curling
3. Red
4. Fencing
5. 3 miles
6. First female cox in the University Boat Race
7. The Saints (the team is Southampton)
8. Four
9. Leicestershire
10. Two

Sport 2 – Answers
1. 36
2. Croquet

3. Gloucestershire
4. Light-heavyweight
5. Nine
6. Joan Benoit (now Samuelson)
7. Cycling
8. Cardiff City
9. 200
10. Rowing, swimming (backstroke) and tug-of-war (but *not* high-jumping, as the rules do not prevent jumpers from going forwards)

Sport 3 – Answers
1. Blackburn Rovers
2. Table Tennis
3. Association Football
4. Don Bradman
5. St. Moritz
6. Basketball
7. Polo
8. Angela Mortimer
9. Cycling
10. 163

Sport 4 – Answers
1. Charlotte Brew
2. Tony Jacklin
3. Nine
4. Sir Gordon Richards
5. Berwick Rangers
6. 1908
7. Two Man Bobsleigh
8. Floyd Patterson
9. Nine
10. Any three from: Crewe Alexandra, Exeter City, Oxford United, Wrexham

Sport 5 – Answers
1. Stirling Moss
2. Queens Park Rangers
3. Three
4. Doncaster (the St. Leger)
5. Melbourne
6. Ice Skating (the International Skating Union)
7. Calcutta Cup
8. 18 (including the coxes)
9. Three
10. Boxing or football (37 and 23 respectively)

Sport 6 – Answers
1. Face-off
2. Queens Park
3. 2 (the other 14 are jumped twice)
4. Badminton
5. Thomas ('The Hitman') Hearns
6. Newcastle United
7. Archery
8. 80 minutes
9. Doncaster
10. One

Sport 7 – Answers
1. Yachting
2. 3,000 metres steeplechase
3. Fred Perry
4. Two
5. Australian Rules Football
6. Lacrosse
7. Badminton
8. 800 metres
9. Exeter City
10. Richard Meade

Sport 8 – Answers
1. Tottenham Hotspur
2. Donald 'Ginger' McCain
3. San Francisco
4. Yorkshire
5. Peter Fleming
6. The F.A. Cup
7. Aston Villa
8. Portugal
9. McLaren
10. John Surtees

Sport 9 – Answers
1. Martin Peters
2. Volleyball
3. Tottenham Hotspur
4. Leicester City
5. Joe Frazier
6. Kiwis (the All Blacks being a Rugby *Union* team)
7. 130 yards
8. Trampolining
9. Tug-of-war
10. 6

Sport & Games – Answers
1. Bridge
2. Canoeing
3. Table tennis
4. Chess
5. Billiards
6. Basketball
7. Marathon
8. Netball
9. Archery
10. Badminton

Television Title Roles – Answers
1. Ian McShane
2. Jon Pertwee
3. Lee Majors

4.   Richard O'Sullivan
5.   Paul Eddington
6.   Raymond Burr
7.   Trevor Eve
8.   James Garner
9.   Peter Falk
10. Gerald Harper

Travel – Answers
1.   Crete
2.   Majorca (accept Mallorca *but not Minorca*)
3.   KLM
4.   Spain
5.   Limerick
6.   Adriatic
7.   Brighton
8.   Switzerland
9.   Iceland
10. Paris

Wars – Answers
1.   World War I ('The Great War')
2.   Boer War
3.   Franco-Prussian War
4.   Korean War
5.   American Civil War
6.   Russo-Japanese War
7.   Crimean War
8.   War of American Independence
9.   Spanish Civil War
10. Opium War

Who? – Answers
1.   Thomas Telford
2.   Mother Teresa
3.   Ibsen
4.   Andropov
5.   Ernest Hemingway

6.   John Wesley
7.   Harold
8.   Calamity Jane
9.   Lord Rutherford
10. Robert Burns

General Knowledge Quick Questions – Answers
1.   Quaver
2.   George Eliot
3.   Pakistan
4.   A.A. Milne
5.   The Lizard
6.   David Niven
7.   Six
8.   Kent
9.   Pluto
10. Lace-making
11. Four
12. Aladdin
13. £800
14. 2001: A Space Odyssey
15. Descartes
16. Charlie Drake
17. Montevideo
18. 50
19. Crimson
20. Budapest
21. 7
22. Italy
23. Irving Berlin
24. Franciscans
25. Salisbury Cathedral
26. Sett
27. Washington Irving
28. O
29. Maggie Smith
30. Abraham
31. 8 yards
32. Italy
33. Pen

34. L. Ron Hubbard
35. Chester
36. Japan
37. Fire
38. Damascus
39. The Pope
40. Victoria
41. 12
42. Victor Hugo
43. Mrs. Hudson
44. Prunella Scales
45. Fidelio
46. Liffey
47. Joanna Lumley
48. Stephen Roche
49. France
50. Milton Keynes
51. Curds and whey
52. River Tiber
53. Sheffield
54. Copenhagen
55. Ten
56. Rabbit
57. 40 years
58. Barbara Castle
59. U.S.A.
60. 23
61. The Oval
62. Venice
63. Evelyn Waugh
64. Manchester City
65. William IV
66. 1896
67. O'Hare
68. Switzerland
69. Alabama
70. Green
71. Grimaldi
72. Mansion House
73. Local Defence Volunteers
74. Four

75. £525
76. Arrows
77. Slade
78. Empire State Building
79. Buck
80. St. Nicholas
81. Kenneth Grahame
82. Dustin Hoffman
83. Uruguay
84. 5 furlongs
85. Batista
86. Sir Barnes Wallis
87. Blackpool
88. Nuffield
89. Paul McCartney
90. Nottingham
91. Llanelli
92. Forging the so-called Hitler
      Diaries
93. Gnasher
94. Bamboo
95. MacDonald
96. Moses
97. Don Quixote
98. Napoleon Bonaparte
99. 72
100. Forget-me-not
101. Two hours
102. Open spaces
103. Dictionaries
104. Thirty years
105. Aries
106. David Broome
107. The Milky Way
108. The ear
109. Four
110. Delaware
111. Mast
112. Parliamentary
      Commissioner For
      Administration

113. Eleven – all bar February
114. Numbers
115. Indian Ocean
116. Aluminium
117. Grace Kelly
118. Twenty-one
119. Eight
120. Sloe
121. Lloyds Bank
122. Virgil
123. Tightrope Walker
124. 1974
125. Ashmolean Museum
126. Twenty-seven
127. Vauxhall
128. Douglas Adams
129. Eight
130. Dior
131. Jean-Claude Killy
132. Argentina
133. August
134. Pipistrelle
135. White
136. Italy
137. Cygnet
138. Dallas
139. Basutoland
140. Calculus
141. Persephone
142. Cancer
143. Liverpool Street
144. Cronus
145. Hen
146. Atlantic City
147. Alabama
148. Mickey Mouse
149. Ben Hur
150. Israel
151. 3
152. H.M.S. Ark Royal
153. Shannon
154. March
155. Alaska
156. Dopey
157. William Cody
158. South Africa
159. Corfu
160. 3 foot
161. St. Andrews
162. Three years
163. Hong Kong
164. Boston
165. Vostok 1
166. Paris
167. Edward VII
168. Iran
169. Thirteen
170. Wisconsin
171. Italy *and* Switzerland
172. The lungs
173. Rome
174. Three
175. Somerset
176. Vienna
177. First Day Cover
178. Tuesday
179. Elephant
180. Marriage
181. 212 degrees
182. The Great Wall of China
183. House of Windsor
184. 720 degrees
185. Lancelot
186. Colchester
187. Eleven inches
188. Palaeontology
189. Eagle
190. Air
191. Four
192. William Blake
193. Belgium
194. Very loud

195. Perth
196. Ampere
197. T.S. Eliot
198. Carmelites
199. Ankara
200. Sir Alec Rose
201. 1997
202. White
203. Zambezi
204. Benjamin Franklin
205. Krishna
206. Ireland
207. Nijinsky
208. A full house
209. Work
210. Edinburgh
211. Lake Coniston
212. Blue
213. Dan Dare
214. Leicestershire
215. Lenin
216. Goebbels
217. Saturday
218. Alexei Leonov
219. Bjorn Borg
220. January 1st (ALL racehorse birthdays are 1st January)
221. France
222. Nicholas II
223. A plum
224. Buckinghamshire
225. Christie
226. Sirhan Sirhan
227. Eros
228. Night vision
229. 20
230. The root
231. St. Denis
232. Thomas Paine
233. Public Sector Borrowing Requirement
234. John Wycliffe
235. 6
236. The Pelican
237. Goose
238. Russia
239. Everything!
240. The Gulf of Bothnia
241. 6
242. Sleeping sickness
243. Norfolk
244. Twenty
245. 2
246. Speedwell
247. 23
248. 4
249. Red
250. Speaker of the House of Commons
251. The Times
252. St. Andrew
253. Blue
254. A bird
255. Sir Humphrey Davy
256. Saturn
257. Buckinghamshire
258. Artificial respiration
259. William Harvey
260. Adrone
261. Kidneys
262. 2
263. St. Louis
264. Cotton
265. Laughing gas
266. Philadelphia
267. Montreal
268. 120
269. Insulin
270. Dutch
271. Henry II
272. Blackbeard
273. Pat Garrett

274. German
275. Prince Philip, Duke of Edinburgh
276. Forties
277. Paris
278. Zambia
279. Trygve Lie
280. Anthony and Cleopatra *or* Romeo and Juliet
281. Lotus
282. Turin
283. Poliomyelitis
284. 50
285. The Hell Fire Club
286. Rowan Atkinson
287. Chile
288. Wine
289. George Harrison ('My Sweet Lord')
290. Daddy-Long-Legs
291. Pretty Maids
292. Salvation Army
293. Femur (the thigh bone)
294. Columbia
295. Snow White and the Seven Dwarfs
296. The Monkees
297. Absolute Zero
298. Eight
299. Hockey
300. Typhoid

Films Quick Questions – Answers
1. Mick Jagger
2. The 'Carry On' films
3. Brief Encounter
4. Richard Attenborough
5. Tasmania
6. The Bates Motel
7. Sean Connery
8. Jack Hawkins
9. The Killing Fields
10. General Custer
11. David Niven
12. Seven
13. Albert Finney
14. The Road To Hong Kong
15. Omar Sharif
16. Queen
17. Peter Cushing
18. Groucho Marx
19. François Truffaut
20. Humphrey Bogart
21. The Wizard of Oz
22. Greta Garbo
23. Sleeping Beauty
24. John Cleese
25. Fred MacMurray
26. Network
27. Sally Bowles
28. Humphrey Bogart
29. Never Say Never Again
30. White Christmas
31. Julie Waters
32. Dooley Wilson
33. Jane Fonda
34. Bob Champion
35. Chariots of Fire
36. A Night to Remember
37. The China Syndrome
38. Edward G. Robinson
39. Beethoven
40. Bill Forsythe
41. Half a Sixpence
42. Loretta Lynn
43. Rosebud
44. Steven Spielberg
45. Cry Freedom
46. Hello, Dolly!
47. Volkswagen
48. Gary Cooper
49. Jean Seberg

50. How Green Was My Valley
51. 1984
52. The Carpetbaggers
53. Pool
54. Sylvester Stallone
55. Gentlemen Marry Brunettes
56. Danish
57. O'Neal (Ryan and Tatum)
58. Bookselling
59. Jewel of the Nile
60. Papillon
61. The Longest Day
62. Passport to Pimlico
63. The Lone Ranger and Tonto
64. Sam Peckinpah
65. Shanghai
66. Kathleen Turner
67. Mark Lester
68. Bette Davis
69. Steve Martin
70. George Lazenby
71. Gerald Scarfe
72. Robert De Niro
73. The African Queen
74. Michael Palin
75. Tom Courtenay
76. The Postman Always Rings Twice
77. Ronald Reagan
78. The Living Daylights
79. King Lear
80. Cynthia Payne
81. Laurence Olivier
82. The Prince and The Showgirl
83. Ice Cold In Alex
84. Key Largo
85. Labyrinth
86. Lady and the Tramp
87. The Thomas Crown Affair
88. Whatever Happened to Baby Jane?
89. Witness
90. Laurence Harvey
91. The Road To Bali
92. Tarzan
93. Robert Mitchum
94. Bonnie and Clyde
95. Arnold Schwarzenegger
96. Ruth Ellis
97. Dorothy
98. White Heat
99. Bing Crosby
100. Smith and Jones

Geography Quick Questions – Answers
1. Spain
2. Namibia
3. Port Said
4. Christchurch
5. Tunisia
6. Bangkok
7. Southampton
8. Indian Ocean
9. North Island and South Island, New Zealand
10. Costa Rica
11. Pyrenees
12. Tanzania
13. River Waveney
14. Australia
15. Volga
16. Germany
17. Brazil
18. Lake Superior
19. The Mariana Trench (the deepest point of which is called Challenger Deep)
20. Donegal
21. Portugal

22.	Ecuador	63.	Bay of Bengal
23.	Moskva	64.	Belfast
24.	Netherlands	65.	Panama Canal
25.	France (it is Mont Blanc)	66.	Japan
26.	The Black Sea	67.	Anticyclone
27.	Albany	68.	Atacama Desert
28.	Cuba	69.	Sierra Leone
29.	New York	70.	Norway
30.	Western Australia	71.	Uruguay
31.	Somerset	72.	Mexico
32.	Leeds	73.	Maine
33.	Malta	74.	Sudan
34.	New Zealand	75.	Salisbury
35.	Brazil	76.	River Tamar
36.	Sudan	77.	Port-Au-Prince
37.	Mt.McKinley	78.	Hawaii
38.	Calm	79.	Orkney Islands
39.	Hungary	80.	Agora
40.	Cumbria	81.	New York
41.	Botswana	82.	South Glamorgan
42.	Essex	83.	Hokkaido
43.	Managua	84.	Sweden
44.	Venezuela	85.	South Australia
45.	San Marino	86.	Iraq
46.	Colorado River	87.	Tonga
47.	Vienna	88.	France
48.	Rome	89.	Australia
49.	Zambezi	90.	Hudson Bay
50.	Tasman Sea	91.	Atlantic Ocean
51.	Ecuador	92.	Northumberland
52.	Lima	93.	Suffolk
53.	German	94.	Laurenço Marques
54.	Poland	95.	Sweden
55.	Zaire River	96.	Kenya
56.	Lake Superior	97.	German
57.	Ecuador	98.	Bridgetown
58.	Tanzania	99.	Sao Paulo
59.	The Philippines	100.	8
60.	Islamabad		
61.	Gobi Desert		
62.	Tallinn		

History Quick Questions –
Answers

1. Richard III
2. Dwight D. Eisenhower
3. Rouen
4. Kublai Khan
5. Rourkes Drift (during the Zulu War)
6. St. Columba
7. James I
8. Martin Luther King
9. Herbert Asquith
10. Russo-Japanese War
11. Chancellor of the Exchequer
12. Witchcraft
13. Copernicus
14. Henry VIII
15. Abraham Lincoln
16. Georges Pompidou
17. U.S.A.
18. Nephew
19. Clement Attlee
20. Culloden
21. 21st Amendment
22. Caernarvon
23. George II
24. Three times
25. General Wolfe
26. Belgium
27. Richard Cromwell
28. Edward VII
29. Sioux
30. Winston Churchill
31. Alexander Dubcek
32. Gibraltar
33. Charles I
34. Rome *and* Carthage
35. Bikini
36. Chicago
37. Malawi
38. Admiral Doenitz
39. The Admiral Graf Spee
40. Italy
41. Great Western
42. John F. Kennedy
43. John Paul I
44. 14th Century
45. Jefferson Davis
46. Venezuela
47. Pizzarro
48. Iceni
49. Battle of Hastings
50. Great Britain
51. Prime Minister
52. James Hargreaves
53. Duke of Marlborough (John Churchill)
54. Louis XVI
55. Robert Clive (later Baron Clive of Plassey)
56. Kublai Khan
57. Lord Mountbatten
58. Woodrow Wilson
59. 600
60. Joachim von Ribbentrop
61. South Korea
62. Haile Selassie
63. Amerigo Vespucci
64. American Civil War
65. Crecy
66. Constantinople
67. Jethro Tull
68. Sir Joseph Thomson
69. Hippocrates
70. Benito Mussolini
71. Benjamin Franklin
72. Joan of Arc
73. Amy Johnson
74. Anwar Sadat
75. Lisbon
76. Austria

77. Falkland Islands
78. King Harold II (though usually remembered as King Harold)
79. Mercia
80. Hawaii
81. Samuel Crompton
82. William Booth
83. Sugar
84. David Lloyd George
85. Leonidas
86. Mexico City
87. Cats' eyes
88. Montezuma
89. Society of Jesus (the Jesuits)
90. Sir Alec Douglas-Home
91. Manchester
92. Troy
93. Russia
94. Piano
95. Jan Smuts
96. Papa Doc
97. Henry VI
98. Sedgemoor
99. Actium
100. John Nash

Literature Quick Questions – Answers

1. Mycroft
2. A.A. Milne
3. Evelyn Waugh
4. Katharina
5. Robinson Crusoe
6. C.S. Lewis
7. Arthur Ransome
8. Isaac Asimov
9. John
10. The Rivals
11. John Fowles
12. Marlowe
13. Vanity Fayre
14. Robot
15. Rosencrantz and Guildenstern
16. Catcher in the Rye
17. Saki
18. Lord Peter Wimsey
19. Peter Shaffer
20. William Shakespeare
21. Timmy
22. George Bernard Shaw
23. Richard Brinsley Sheridan
24. Alan Sillitoe
25. Beachcomber
26. Benjamin Disraeli
27. Fourteen
28. Hercule Poirot
29. J.M. Barrie
30. John Buchan
31. Heathcliff
32. Spike Milligan
33. Under Milk Wood
34. Ulysses
35. Oscar Wilde
36. Five
37. Westminster Bridge
38. Xanadu
39. John Wyndham
40. Jeffrey Archer
41. The Water Babies
42. Samuel Beckett
43. Beatrix Potter
44. George Orwell
45. Edith Nesbit
46. Albatross
47. Jim Hawkins
48. Frances Hodgson Burnett
49. Tom Sharpe
50. Thirteen and three-quarters
51. Clergy (of the Church of England)

52. Dove Cottage
53. Brobdingnag
54. German
55. H.E. Bates
56. Far From the Madding Crowd
57. 24
58. Robert Louis Stevenson
59. The Importance of Being Earnest
60. Minnehaha
61. Trinidad
62. Twelfth Night
63. Boz
64. R.D. Blackmore
65. Anthony Trollope
66. Salvation Army
67. George Eliot
68. John Keats
69. Norman Mailer
70. The Tempest
71. John Osborne
72. Hard Times
73. Penguin
74. Lewis Carroll
75. Anne Hathaway
76. Pride and Prejudice
77. Anthony Burgess
78. Leonard Cohen
79. Branwell
80. Siegfried Sassoon
81. Dennis Potter
82. Wilfred Owen
83. Paul Scott
84. Sancho Panza
85. Nevil Shute
86. Capulet
87. Robert Graves
88. Lord Chamberlain
89. Captain W.E. Johns
90. Bysshe

91. T.S. Eliot
92. Captain Flint
93. George Smiley
94. The Prisoner of Zenda
95. Dryden
96. Admiral Benbow
97. Dostoevsky
98. Edgar Rice Burroughs
99. Lamb (Charles and Mary)
100. Desdemona

Music Quick Questions – Answers
1.   Bee Gees
2.   Ringo Starr
3.   Sadlers Wells Opera
4.   Poland
5.   Harmonica
6.   Earth and Pluto
7.   The Dakotas
8.   Col. Tom Parker
9.   Igor Stravinsky
10. Mick Taylor
11. French
12. The Mindbenders
13. Jacques Offenbach
14. French
15. Phil Collins
16. A cappella
17. Mikis Theodorakis
18. Moody Blues
19. Parsifal
20. The Emperor Concerto
21. David Bowie
22. Sir Benjamin Britten
23. The Beach Boys
24. Mezzo-soprano
25. The Beatles
26. Elvis Presley
27. Duke Ellington
28. Paul Anka
29. Puccini

30. Penny Lane
31. Aida
32. Thompson Twins
33. East Sussex
34. Merry Xmas Everbody
35. Largo
36. The Rolling Stones
37. Ryan (Marion and Barry)
38. Mozart
39. Organ
40. Isaac Hayes
41. Quadrophenia
42. Verdi
43. Israel (though usually known as Ira)
44. Georgie Fame
45. Metropolitan Opera House (often referred to as the 'Met')
46. Sophia Loren
47. Manfred Mann
48. Bach
49. The Bandwagon
50. Living Doll

Radio and Television Quick Questions – Answers

1. Perry Mason
2. Weatherfield
3. Michael Parkinson
4. Till Death Us Do Part
5. Greendale
6. The Mary Tyler Moore Show
7. Parker
8. Ready Steady Go
9. The Archers
10. Bill Simpson
11. Robert Lindsay
12. Jimmy Edwards
13. Warmington-on-Sea
14. Tom O'Connor
15. Happy Days
16. Petra
17. University Challenge
18. Boston
19. Red Dwarf
20. Steve Austin
21. Arthur Marshall
22. Steve Zodiac
23. Leo McKern
24. Graham Kerr
25. The Waltons
26. Chips
27. Fenn Street
28. Alistair Cooke
29. Time and Relative Dimensions in Space
30. Barry Foster
31. Sorry
32. Paula Wilcox
33. Charlie Hungerford
34. BBC 2
35. Hercules
36. Mycroft
37. Montreux
38. Jimmy Savile
39. Alfred Burke
40. Dr. Kildare
41. Carla Lane
42. The Man in Black
43. Lost in Space
44. Shaw Taylor
45. James Herriot
46. Juke Box Jury
47. Watts
48. Rising Damp
49. Coronation Street
50. Patrick Troughton

Science Quick Questions –
Answers
1. Eye
2. He
3. Liver
4. Vitamin C
5. Red
6. Pancreas
7. W
8. Lead
9. Germany
10. Osteopathy
11. Henry
12. Cyprus
13. Methane
14. Hydrogen
15. Ultrasonics
16. Random Access Memory
17. Au
18. Troposphere
19. Jupiter
20. Computer
21. Elephant
22. Nitrogen
23. None!
24. Nylon
25. PVC
26. Enrico Fermi
27. James Joyce
28. Tungsten
29. A yard
30. Helium
31. Venus
32. Arsenic
33. 640
34. Cumberland – now Cumbria
35. Corundum
36. Quinine
37. Mars
38. Saint Elmo's Fire
39. Aspirin
40. Trapezium
41. Methane
42. Stamen
43. Carbon dioxide
44. A kidney
45. Vitamin K
46. Windscale
47. Sirocco
48. Chromium
49. Chloroform
50. Sir Humphrey Davy

Sport Quick Questions – Answers
1. Backstroke
2. India
3. Kentucky Derby
4. Four
5. Squash
6. Chamonix
7. Fifteen
8. Stockholm (quarantine precautions prevented them from taking place at Melbourne)
9. 12 feet
10. 1500 metres
11. Butterfly
12. June
13. London Marathon
14. Cycling
15. Golf
16. Alain Prost
17. Tourist Trophy
18. Six
19. Greg LeMond
20. Blue
21. One
22. Blackpool and Stoke City
23. Marylebone Cricket Club
24. Twenty-four
25. Ireland

26. Bob Fitzsimmons
27. Edinburgh
28. Maiden
29. Six
30. Mark Spitz
31. St. Leger
32. Swimming
33. Orienteering
34. Four
35. Judo
36. Tony Jacklin
37. Garfield (Gary) Sobers
38. Billie Jean King
39. Rifle shooting
40. Sabre
41. Three
42. British Open Golf
43. Six
44. Tony Roche
45. Four
46. Pelota
47. 22 yards
48. Light-flyweight
49. Jacques Anquetil *or* Bernard Hinault *or* Eddy Mercx *or* Miguel Indurain
50. Golf

'Gamble' Questions – Answers

A. Sir Winston Churchill
B. Missouri
C. Abraham Lincoln
D. Stan Laurel
E. Charles Dickens
F. Sir Christopher Wren
G. Morocco
H. W.C. Fields
I. Paul Newman

Table Questions 1 – Capital Cities – Answers

1. Tirana
2. Buenos Aires
3. Canberra
4. Brasilia
5. Sofia
6. Ottawa
7. Santiago
8. Copenhagen
9. Accra
10. Athens
11. Teheran
12. Baghdad
13. Nairobi
14. Vientiane
15. Tripoli
16. Vaduz
17. Rabat
18. Wellington
19. Kathmandu
20. Lagos
21. Panama City
22. Riyadh
23. Berne
24. Ankara
25. Hanoi

Table Question 2 – Years – Answers

A	–	1961
B	–	1966
C	–	1969
D	–	1971
E	–	1979
F	–	1977
G	–	1963
H	–	1973
I	–	1962
J	–	1974
K	–	1978
L	–	1967
M	–	1964

N	–	1970
O	–	1972
P	–	1975
Q	–	1965
R	–	1968
S	–	1976
T	–	1960

Table Question 3 – Countries – Answers

1. Ghana
2. Ethiopia
3. Sri Lanka
4. Belize
5. Zambia
6. South Yemen
7. Guyana
8. Zaire
9. Burkina Faso
10. Saudi Arabia
11. Iran
12. Bangladesh
13. Malawi
14. Djibouti
15. Guinea–Bissau
16. Mali
17. Zimbabwe
18. Surinam
19. Thailand
20. Indonesia

Table Question 4 – Film Anagrams – Answers

1. Psycho
2. Goldfinger
3. The Third Man
4. Brighton Rock
5. Gone With The Wind
6. The Maltese Falcon
7. The Great Dictator
8. Brief Encounter
9. Robocop
10. The Great Escape
11. A Fish Called Wanda
12. The Godfather
13. Out of Africa
14. Key Largo
15. The Magnificent Seven
16. Moonstruck
17. Carry On Constable
18. Last Tango in Paris
19. Platoon
20. Fort Apache

Table Question 5 – Which County? – Answers

1. Dorset
2. Suffolk
3. Somerset
4. Leicestershire
5. Cheshire
6. Wiltshire
7. Staffordshire
8. Kent
9. Hampshire
10. Merseyside
11. Bedfordshire
12. Oxfordshire
13. Northamptonshire
14. Cleveland
15. Hertfordshire
16. Berkshire
17. Cambridgeshire
18. Cornwall
19. Warwickshire
20. Derbyshire

Table Question 6 – Olympic Venues – Answers

1. London
2. Helsinki
3. Melbourne

4. Rome
5. Tokyo
6. Mexico City
7. Munich
8. Montreal
9. Moscow
10. Los Angeles
11. Seoul
12. Barcelona

Table Question 7 – Sports – Answers

1. Bowls
2. Speedway
3. Squash
4. Rifle Shooting
5. Table Tennis
6. Archery
7. Badminton
8. Swimming
9. Motor Cycling
10. Judo
11. Ice Skating
12. Darts
13. Modern Pentathlon
14. Motor Racing
15. Snooker
16. Cycling
17. Gymnastics
18. Diving
19. Billiards

20. Water Skiing

Table Question 8 – Pop Music – Answers

1. Billy Ocean
2. The Platters
3. Abba
4. Doris Day
5. Ricky Valance
6. Paul Hardcastle
7. Anita Ward
8. Jimmy Young
9. Adam and the Ants
10. Gilbert O'Sullivan
11. The Troggs
12. Joe Dolce
13. The Shadows
14. Tight Fit
15. Donny Osmond
16. Matthews Southern Comfort
17. Buggles
18. A-Ha
19. Blondie
20. Charles Aznavour
21. The Flying Pickets
22. Des O'Connor
23. David Soul
24. Paper Lace
25. Pet Shop Boys

Table Question 9 – 'Call My Bluff' – Answers

A. (Aliform) b) wing-shaped
B. (Baryon) c) an elementary particle
C. (Catchpole) a) a medieval officer who arrested debtors
D. (Digamy) a) a second marriage
E. (Euphotic) c) the uppermost part of a sea or lake
F. (Friable) b) crumbly

G. (Guck)   a) slimy matter
H. (Hoggin)   c) finely sifted gravel
I.   (Ichnite)   a) a fossilized footprint
J.   (Jukskei)   c) a South African game
K. (Kokako)   b) a New Zealand wattled crow
L. (Lincrusta)   a) a type of wallpaper
M. (Midiron)   c) a No. 2 iron used in golf
N. (Nipa)   c) a pine tree
O. (Orogeny)   a) the formation of mountain ranges
P. (Pomelo)   c) a citrus fruit
Q. (Qindar)   b) an Albanian unit of currency
R. (Restharrow)   a) a plant with woody stems and roots
S. (Scow)   a) a freight-barge
T. (Teocalli)   a) a truncated Aztec pyramid
U. (Ursine)   b) bear-like
V. (Vigoro)   b) an Australian women's game like cricket
W. (Withershins)   b) anticlockwise
X. (Xerosis)   c) abnormal dryness of bodily tissues
Y. (Yulan)   a) a Chinese magnolia
Z. (Zander)   b) a fish

QUIRKY QUIZ QUESTIONS
by John Bates

You don't have to be an expert to be a contender in this quiz book from John Bates. A unique quiz that challenges the old with a ground-breaking format. Bates brings to his quiz a particular sense of humour and style that covers a range of subjects within themes. By blurring the distinctions of subject within a main theme the quiz becomes a test for the agile of mind. From 2,500 questions you can expect to encounter a diversity of categories, from vegetables to the human body, with questions of both a popular and classical nature.

A quiz book that guarantees an original contest.

READY-MADE QUIZZES
by Bill Murray

Can't face compiling a set of questions and organising them into a sensible order? Then the answer is at hand. This book will take all the hard work out of running a quiz. Questions are organised into two sorts of quiz: individual (table) quizzes and team (league) quizzes. The questions have been carefully sorted to ensure that each team has questions of comparable difficulty. No team should cry bias if you use this book. You'll no longer have to search through libraries to compile questions with this collection. Ideal for *all* quiz contests!

THE QUIZ-SETTER'S QUIZ BOOK
by Don Wilson

No matter how well organized a quiz evening is, unless there are plenty of questions for the team members to tackle it won't be much fun — and a good quiz takes up a surprisingly large volume of questions. Don Wilson has carefully compiled 2,000+ questions into rounds that are straightforward to use. With the answers right beside the questions this is the book you've all been waiting for!

HOW TO SOLVE
CRYPTIC CROSSWORDS
by Kevin Skinner

This is the book for you if you cannot understand how Cryptic Crosswords work. In it, experienced cryptic crossword compiler and solver Kevin Skinner explains all the various sorts of clue you are likely to encounter and shows you how to recognise each type and how to solve them. And there are example crosswords to try, with answers given *and explained*, for you to check your progress.

BEGIN BRIDGE
by G C H Fox

Written by *The Daily Telegraph's* former Bridge correspondent, this book delves into the heart of each skill that the beginner needs and explains each difficulty in terms that everyone can understand.

"A clear and reliable introduction for the complete beginner."
Terence Reese in *The Observer*

"Outlines clearly the basic principles of bidding, play and defence."
R A Priday in *The Sunday Telegraph*

THE RIGHT WAY TO
PLAY BRIDGE

The complete reference to successful Acol bidding
and the key principles of play
* for improving players *

This book assumes that you are intent on improving your bridge at a social, or competitive, level. Clear examples expose the detail of modern Acol bidding. Unique at-the-table charts – designed to foster partnership understanding used appropriately at home, club or class – summarise key bids.

Paul Mendelson is a bridge professional at the Roehampton Club and teaches throughout London and is a keen tournament competitor.

RIGHT WAY
PUBLISHING POLICY

HOW WE SELECT TITLES
RIGHT WAY consider carefully every deserving manuscript. Where an author is an authority on his subject but an inexperienced writer, we provide first-class editorial help. The standards we set make sure that every **RIGHT WAY** book is practical, easy to understand, concise, informative and delightful to read. Our specialist artists are skilled at creating simple illustrations which augment the text wherever necessary.

CONSISTENT QUALITY
At every reprint our books are updated where appropriate, giving our authors the opportunity to include new information.

FAST DELIVERY
We sell **RIGHT WAY** books to the best bookshops throughout the world. It may be that your bookseller has run out of stock of a particular title. If so, he can order more from us at any time – we have a fine reputation for "same day" despatch, and we supply any order, however small (even a single copy), to any bookseller who has an account with us. We prefer you to buy from your bookseller, as this reminds him of the strong underlying public demand for **RIGHT WAY** books. Readers who live in remote places, or who are housebound, or whose local bookseller is unco-operative, can order direct from us by post.

FREE
If you would like an up-to-date list of all **RIGHT WAY** titles currently available, send a stamped self-addressed envelope to
ELLIOT RIGHT WAY BOOKS, BRIGHTON RD.,
LOWER KINGSWOOD, TADWORTH, SURREY, KT20 6TD,U.K.
or visit our web site at www.right-way.co.uk